No Stamps On My Passport

by

Ken Roberts

Hope Adrian

The long search paid off

All the best

Ken. Roberts

No Stamps On My Passport

by

Ken Roberts

Published by
Mediaworld PR Ltd
Best Books Online

First paperback edition published in Great Britain
June 2007 by
Best Books Online
Mediaworld PR Ltd

ISBN: 978-1-904502-99-9

Printed and bound by CPI Antony Rowe, Eastbourne

Acknowledgements

For **Clive**, he never got this far.

For **Vicky** and **Hugh** who I lost
and
For **Wendy** and **Kirk**, for putting up with me.

Chapter One
FIRST MEMORIES

My early childhood is something of a mist to me now, but a mist that is not entirely thick, some memories are vivid, some not. I was born in 1949 in a small welsh town called Llandrindod Wells in the county that was then Radnorshire, now, due to government reorganisation, it is the county town of Powys.

The town, Victorian in its architecture, rests in a valley in mid Wales it is sadly run down although it still stands as a monument to the Victorian era, both in structure and in attitudes. Unfortunately time for the greater part has stood still any attempt to drag the town into the present day fails due to a lack of enthusiasm, the fear of hard work and investment. Many have tried and failed only to move on to pastures new and, I am sure, far greener.

It has made some inroads to improve its image by turning back the clock and introducing more Victorian restoration, including a Victorian festival for two weeks of the year, this has had a modicum of success over the years but alas even that has become rather jaded, sort of progress by retreat. There have been many attempts to improve the town only for them to be rejected by the local mafia.

I now find the town uninviting, it was my birthplace, but it has over the years lost its character, along with its appeal therefore I visit less and less. I feel very sad about this but I have moved on, the town has not.

My first memory of home was a shared house at the lower end of town, the house did not get a lot of sunlight due to the fact it was on the edge of the park facing a forest of trees that shaded the light casting a forbidding shadow over the house for most of the day.

When autumn winds blew the trees would blow and creak, leaves would rustle and whisper messages across to the house. I would lie awake trying to make out what messages they were trying to convey, maybe they were telling me winter was on the way and to wrap up warm against the cold wind that was due any time. My young life seemed to be made up of winters. I can never remember feeling warm, I still suffer from the cold, probably due to the fact I was never warm as a child. When the storms of winter came, the leaves would fall to the ground and block the drains in the road causing great puddles of water to seep under the house this caused the house to be damp and cold, although it did provide a wet playground and lots of splashing games were played in those mini lakes.

The house called Oakley Villa was in a street called Park Crescent, an old damp house very dark and unfriendly. It smelt damp and musty, the walls were always cold and damp to the touch, the windows never smiled or sparkled, the house never said welcome, it had attitude, it never welcomed us home, it seemed to have a life; a life that breathed dark damp breath as the front door opened. When entered it inhaled you into its cold, brick body, you felt trapped, the front door half-frosted glass, was painted council green, the same colour green which adorned most of the seats in the park. There was a big dirty brass doorknob, which was never cleaned, it had tinges of green and felt rough to the touch much like sandpaper, not like the doorknob on the house up the road that gleamed gold, in what little sun reflected onto it. I wanted to clean our doorknob but was told to leave it alone, it wasn't hurting anyone, of course it wouldn't hurt anyone it was a doorknob. The letterbox was the same, green with no spring to keep it closed, this used to rattle in the wind and very often had to be stuck down with tape to stop the clatter when the wind blew.

The doorbell was worked by pulling a chain, which looked like it came out of a lavatory, it probably did. This chain in turn was attached to a large coiled spring by means of a wire chord, the bell being attached to this spring, the whole assembly was fastened to the wall in the passage way, it would fall off the wall most every time someone pulled the chain, consequently after a time it took up permanent residence on the floor.

All the windows were a sash cord system, these were never opened, no fresh air entered through the windows, most of which were cracked and needed replacing. The main passageway into the house was long and dark, the floor was quarry tiled covered by a carpet runner, which slipped if you were not careful, but it was home, or part home.

We were kept warm most of the time by an Aladdin paraffin heater with a large round steel mesh burner which glowed bright orange, blue and red. When the kitchen door was opened a draught made it splutter, telling us to close the door, this heater was the focal point in the kitchen, it burned all day and gurgled when a fresh supply of pink paraffin was delivered to the burner. The smell of that stove was terrible, it made your eyes sting and your nose itch, until you got used to it. It took a long time to warm the kitchen.

I was four years old, when we lived in Oakley Villa, and even now I can walk my way around that old miserable house. I remember every door and window, there were thirteen stairs to the upstairs rooms, then a further four stairs up to the top landing.

When I returned to Llandrindod years later I wanted to buy Oakley Villa and knock it down as it held so many bad memories, but this was a dream never to be fulfilled, however, there is still time.

We had lived at my Nana's house for a while, although I can't remember much of that, it was the top floor of an old hotel converted into flats called Temple Lodge. My father and Nana could not get on, so we had to move out before murder was committed, she would have murdered him given half a chance.

The other occupant, who actually owned Oakley Villa, was an elderly man, Mr. Wilkins. He was not a nice man, he was always grumpy and shouted at me a lot for making a noise, my father called him the old sod. I was told to keep out of his way and never go into his room, I suppose he was what is known today as a paedophile, but words that long were not invented then, he was a dirty old man, one of the dirty raincoat brigade, a fiddler.

He would creep around and appear in doorways, never saying a word, just staring, this led to lots of arguments between mother and father. Mother was frightened for our safety and wanted to get us out of the house, she was afraid of this man, we spent many hours a day either at my Nana's or walking about town.

Father was only earning five pounds a week, working at a tuberculosis hospital as a maintenance engineer. Money was tight, times were hard, rows were frequent. He had a sort of Saturday job with a local pig breeder, Arthur Stevenson. I sometimes went to see the pigs and helped with the feeding and cleaning the styes, he got paid thirty bob, for that, it came to be known as the thirty bob job.

The hospital, father worked at was at the far end of town on the road to Builth Wells, it was known as Highland Moors. I have vague memories of this huge building, it has always reminded me of a prison, it probably felt that way to the poor unfortunates who found themselves too ill to move. Later in the sixties and seventies it was a convent, then left empty for a few years before being converted into a hotel. It was a four mile bike ride and father used to cycle to work each day rain or shine. He caught fire once cycling down the road, he put what he thought was his unlit pipe in his jacket pocket but it was not out, wind fanned the embers causing his jacket to catch fire, he was burning quite well before he realised he was on fire, mother threw a bowl of water on him to put him out, he gave up smoking after that incident.

Sharing a house had many restrictions we had to share rooms. Our side of the living room was by the front window, which afforded us a view of the park, although all we saw were trees. The room had a fireplace, a sideboard where some toys were kept and a sofa and two easy chairs covered in mock leather. We could light a fire in this room if we wished, it was not lit very often, coal was expensive and on father's wages it was not on the list of priorities. So most of the winter months were spent in the kitchen with the Aladdin heater. On the mantelpiece sat an old clock, along with a few of mother's ornaments, two candlesticks and a green glass vase. The front room was reasonably warm and comfortable, though when the old sod was in the room, noise had to be kept to a minimum. He was always reading a newspaper, he never went anywhere without a newspaper. He would be up at six every morning and would crash around the kitchen, before father came down at six-thirty, then he would return to his room until father had gone to work never saying a word.

We shared the kitchen, it was very difficult to move freely for fear of upsetting the old sod, so meals had to be timed so he could use the cooker and sink. He had his own food cupboard that was locked with a padlock, he would keep his cooking utensils along with his dishes in this cupboard. There was a gas stove and a stone sink, we were bathed in this every Sunday when father had to sit by the kitchen door for fear the old sod would come in. There was a meat safe, this was a perforated tin cabinet that was fitted into the wall, milk, butter and meat were stored here and the flow of air through the perforations would, in theory, keep whatever was stored, fresh and away from flies. It had a padlock to stop things disappearing, as mother used to say, I thought things disappeared by magic and the padlock stopped the magic. There was also a table and chairs, and a tall cupboard where other food was stored, this also had a padlock to stop the magic.

We had two bedrooms, one of which I shared with my sister, she was two years younger than me. She had bright ginger hair and a temper to match, she once won an orange juice competition for being a pretty baby and she had a knack for getting her own way, she was spoiled by everyone who saw her. She would also cry a lot, this upset the old sod. She fell down the stairs one day and the old sod just stepped over her, went into the living room and sat down, shouting at mother to 'shut that kid up'.

There were four bedrooms in the house. Mr Wilkins occupied two, one for sleeping and one with a big padlock on the door. I never found out what magic he kept in that room. This part of his house was strictly out of bounds the house was full of padlocks, but not much magic.

The main bedroom had a veranda, which looked out onto the

park, this was where mother and father slept. We were told never to go onto this veranda as it was not safe, though I used to creep out and watch people walk by.

The garden at the rear of the house was large and well kept. Father was a very keen gardener and grew all sorts of vegetables. I hated vegetables especially cabbage, and I still do, but in the garden there seemed to be a never-ending supply of this disgusting green leaf. Peas, beans, lettuce, carrots and potatoes were also grown, and in a small greenhouse; tomatoes.

The garden backed onto the main mid Wales railway line where there were wild raspberries and blackberries, we used to pick these, getting badly scratched in the process, but it was worth it, eating as we picked, covering our mouths and clothes in purple and red stains.

I used to sit on the wooden style father had built to get at the allotment he had taken over which ran along the railway and watch the steam trains go by, belching smoke, and steam, huffing and puffing like a huge animal gasping for breath. At night, looking out of the kitchen window, you could see sparks coming out of the firebox. Sometime the embankments would be set on fire and the fire brigade would be called to put it out, this would add much excitement, and worry about the blackberry bushes and the allotment being destroyed, but things always grew back bigger and stronger.

The park was vast a jungle of trees, shrubs and hideaways, at the lower end there were bowling greens, the pride of the town, these were very well kept and managed. Tournaments were, and are, still played on them every year bringing bowlers from all over the country to compete. There were tennis courts, a dance hall and a spa where people came to drink the waters, which were supposed to have healing qualities. The water, sulphurous in taste, sold for a penny a glass, they at best made you vomit quite violently, so none of the locals took them, although visitors from all over the world vomited quite freely and maintained they felt much better after the event.

The park gardens were a wonderful sight, the flowers and

rhododendron bushes were stunningly beautiful, flower beds, were meticulously cared for by an army of four gardeners in the employ of the council, for all the lack of manpower the park in full bloom was a magnificent sight. Pinks and deep reds were the prominent colour, followed closely by yellow and gold. Primroses and bluebells in the spring, winter pansies flowering trees with all colours of blossom, wild cherry, crab apple and a host of others. Picking flowers was not allowed but a few found their way into the green glass vase on the mantelpiece. There were roses of all varieties and colours, hundreds of shrubs, I never knew the name of, a huge variety of trees, oaks, ash, birch, willow, hazel, yew, sycamore, horse chestnut and many more. We made bows out of the yew and arrows out of the hazel, in the autumn we collected conkers, and leaves to press into books for school projects.

Wildlife was in abundance with birds, rabbits, foxes, squirrels and pheasants. Some were considered pests but I could never see that any animal was a pest. I once watched hares boxing, I watched them for what seemed like hours, it was a wonderful sight, to see wild animals so frequently they were almost taken for granted. I considered them as wild pets and would spend many hours trying to get closer to them, some were even given names and could be recognised by their markings.

The local pest control officer, Tom Lloyd, was paid a bounty on grey squirrels and rats that used to infest the streams that ran through the park. I did not like rats but I hated to see him killing squirrels, he could often be heard shooting with either his shotgun or rifle somewhere in the woods, he would often shoot wood pigeons, rabbits and the occasional pheasant for the pot. We used to try to frighten the squirrels to stop him shooting them but with little success, he would chase us off threatening to shoot us instead of them! He got paid sixpence a tail, in those days it was good money, Tom, also looked after the local boating lake where I spent many hours fishing and boating. In winter we would sit around a pot bellied stove in the boathouse listening to Tom tell tales and help repair the boats, we were probably more of a nuisance than a help but Tom seemed to like the company. It also got us a few free goes on the boats. On the whole Tom was a countryman who had been trapped in town but did his best to keep his country ways, passing on to us youngsters who were interested enough to listen, tips on looking after nature and all her wonders.

I had a favourite tree in the park, a Wellentonia, it still stands at the entrance to the park, I used to punch the trunk as hard as I could, its bark was very soft. I would punch my tree when I had been in trouble, it eased the tension, and it did not punch back, it was well over a hundred feet tall and very beautiful.

The stream that flowed through the park had started its long fall from the River Ithon at a place called Shaky Bridge, over ten miles away, it cut through the town by means of tunnels and bridges where it ended its journey rejoining the River Ithon at the bottom end of the park. I have walked this stream many times, often taking a drink from its clear waters, then walking upstream a hundred yards only to find a dead sheep lying in the same water. I never got ill from drinking the stream water, but the next time I would walk the stream I would remember where I saw the dead sheep and drink from upstream only to find another one further up; sod's law.

The stream on its passage through the town is mostly through culverts but occasionally it reappears to form part of a feature in the town, one such place was what is locally known as the recreation grounds. This was where the library was housed before being moved to an old hotel that had gone out of business. There was a bandstand where I would, in my secondary school days, sneak off for a smoke - out of sight out of mind.

The towns war memorial is situated in the grounds and is very well cared for, it is a statue of a soldier of the Great War 1914/18. He stands looking at the main A483 road with his gun barrel down, his hands crossed on the butt, his head bowed, he stands on a tall white plinth, a memorial to all who lost their lives, in two wars.

Several smaller streams break away from the arterial flow, each taking its own course through the park, sometimes muddy sometimes clear, depending on how much rain had fallen, washing soil off fields and banks into the streams. Shaded by trees and shrubs, often disappearing into the undergrowth, then suddenly reappearing into the sunlight, flashing, rushing, cutting through rock gorges to the river, over rocks and through pools, over waterfalls, always in a hurry, gurgling and splashing then at last into the River Ithon once again, then onward to the River Wye.

One small part of the stream was said to have healing properties, a small triangular section was sectioned off during the Victorian era and a concrete platform laid for easy access. This small section of water, trapped in the triangle, was said to be able to cure some sort of eye disease, but I never knew anybody who had been cured.

At one point the stream runs through a tunnel, it must be two hundred yards long and very dark, water would constantly drip from the roof and if you shouted down this long black corridor, an echo came back and sounded even louder than you shouted. As kids we would dare each other to walk through it, there was supposed to be a very deep hole in the tunnel, but I never went through to find out, I was terrified of small dark places.

Following the stream you will eventually come to lover's leap, where I used to fish. This was a huge rock formation it was said that lovers who were not allowed to marry would throw themselves off this rock into the whirlpool below. I never saw the whirlpool except when the river was in full flood and the water a muddy brown. I could never understand why anybody would want to jump into muddy water, even for love.

The river was grossly over fished but if you knew where the fish were, you could catch a reasonable brown trout and sometimes hook into a salmon, this would give a good fight and if you were very skilful you could land one and sell it to the local hotels. The water bailiff, Mr Brown, would often patrol the river looking for fishermen without licences, if you knew the river it was easy to hide, if he caught you he would take your fishing tackle and confiscate it. Bastard.

There were miles of pathways and walks, plenty of hiding places, all sorts of trees to climb. This park was and still is a very pleasant place and I hope it will remain so for many years, but planners being what they are, I very much doubt it.

The local cinema, The Grand Pavilion, was at the top of the park next to the Holy Trinity Church the largest church in town, where I would in future years attend many weddings and funerals. The Grand Pavilion was far from grand, it had been neglected for many years and most of it was crumbling but it still showed three films a week. It was a very busy place during the war years and was full every night, my mother worked there as an usherette during the war. It was here I first saw my favourite film *Zulu* with Stanley Baker and Michael Cain. Each Saturday morning there would be a matinee showing such films as *The Three Stooges, Davy Crockett*, *Rocket Man* and many other heroes. After the Saturday matinees, scores of wild kids would make for the park to act out what they had seen on the flicks. Uncontrolled mayhem would ensue.

The park was an adventure playground used by generations before us, but I doubt not to many generations behind us.

~*~

At the end of our road (Park Crescent) stood a building called the Gwalia, the council offices, where various government departments could be found. It was where you went to tax your car, look at plans or register births, marriages and deaths. It was the most impressive building in town and if you worked there you were deemed to be important, you probably owned your own house. The entrance had a revolving door, which led into a highly decorated foyer, there were several offices on the ground floor as well as the council chamber, then a staircase led to the offices on the upper level; planning and the health department.

When you are very small this was a magnificent place, as you get older however you start to see all the cracks and not only in the building. There were lots of underhand dealing went on behind closed doors. I always found the revolving door a challenge as you had to keep walking in a circle, much as many who worked there had to.

The local grocer's shop was known as 'Bouncing Bob's'. Bob was a very round man always smiling, his shop was spotlessly clean and very welcoming. Bob had lost some fingers off one of his hands, I can't remember which hand, but he would always tell me he had chopped them off in the bacon slicer. This finger slicer occupied the end of the main counter, it was a hand cranked Berkell model, big and red. I used to turn the handle sometimes, it was very heavy and you had to get it up to speed to slice the bacon which would fly out of the side of the big revolving blade to be caught very deftly and neatly stacked on some greaseproof paper then taken to the scales to be weighed. The bacon would come in huge sides wrapped in cloth, it had to be jointed and cut to size before it would fit onto the slicer. Years later when I had my own delicatessen I had a slicer just like Bob's, each time I used it I remembered Bob's fingers and took my time.

There were rows of biscuit tins with all different varieties; *Huntley and Palmer, Jacobs, Peek Freens.* All these tins were on a stand the whole length of the counter some had lids with glass tops so you could see what was inside, some had no lids at all. Bob would let us, when we went into the shop with our mother, take two biscuits only, this was a treat, and we would try and get mum to shop every day so we could have a dip in the tins, my favourites were fig rolls and custard creams, my tastes haven't changed. The smell of that shop - fresh coffee, (we never had real coffee we had Camp chicory essence which was very nice made with ideal milk), bread and cheese, cooked meats, tinned goods and all sorts of baking paraphernalia, an Aladdin's cave of food. A shop such as Bob's would never be allowed today, the health and safety would see to that, although nobody seemed to get food poisoning or upsets as they do today.

Next to Bouncing Bob's was a chemist called, Shewens, although the sign above the door was Johnson & Johnson. In the window were huge onion shaped, glass bottles, filled with all sorts of coloured liquid, these would catch the sunlight which then reflected inside the chemist, casting long coloured shapes along the walls. There was a weighing scales, mother would put a penny in the slot and weigh me, I thought this was for fun but it was to check I was putting on weight. I was very thin, they called me a sickly child, I was forced to wear short trousers these did not help my appearance, I took on the appearance of a matchstick man. I hated short trousers they were draughty and cold.

Inside the shop a long glass counter was filled with such things as cough medicine and tablets for headaches, plasters, bandages, powders for this and that. Such an array of medicines and cures for every ailment, if you were poorly the chemist would give you a draft of medicine to make you better, usually castor oil or a peppermint tasting thick liquid to settle your stomach, or some such potion. Behind the counter the whole wall was covered with small draws, each had a white label with strange words, indicating what medicines they contained, and a ladder that ran on a rail the whole length of the counter in order that the chemist could reach to the top shelf.

Further up the road was a newsagent and fishing tackle shop owned by two brothers, (I bought my first gun from this shop), a butcher, a sweet shop and tobacconist, and a bakers, we were well catered for in the way of shops in our little part of town, and had no need to stray from our neighbourhood. Unfortunately today this part of town is very run down with hardly a shop that isn't boarded up, thanks to the council and a new supermarket. Another forward step! Backwards.

~*~

My parents fought a lot, mostly about money or the lack of it, my mother had no control over the purse strings, as money came in so it went out, my father had a foul temper, and when he was annoyed, mostly because of the shortage of money, everyone kept well out of his way. He would lose control over the slightest thing, he would shout and throw things around sometimes he would get so mad his eyes would glaze over and he would pass out, this did not happen very often, but he did get mad a lot. I used to hide with my sister, who was just a baby, in a cupboard under the stairs until he settled down. This was a dark safe place and we used to stay there until mother got us out, it was our shelter, my sister would cry all the time we were in there but it was the safest place to be.

One of my first memories of the terrible rows at Oakley Villa was tripping over a bucket that had been thrown, by father at mother, up the passageway. I tripped over this bucket trying to escape and split my head open, I was four years old, and I still carry the scar. It itches from time to time, reminding me that I was not fast enough. I can remember the hospital and the stinging pain when iodine was applied, but not much after, I always dived for the stair cupboard after that, dragging my sister behind me.

I had a three wheeled tricycle, it was green and had no mudguards they had long fallen off but I treasured it, it was given to me by a family who had moved from next door, their sons had grown out of it, it was my pride and joy I loved it. I used to race so fast I was always crashing into things. When I was five years old I was knocked off my three-wheel trike, by a pick up truck, driven by a local builder, George Smith, he was a kind man who never forgot this incident. I learned from his wife years later that he could not sleep for months after the accident he would sit up most nights afraid to close his eyes, he told her he was reliving the crash every time he closed his eyes. I was probably trying to emulate Geoff Duke, he was a motorcycle racer who won the Isle of Man TT motorcycle races in 1951. I never saw him but he was always talked about, so I adopted him as my hero, he had a great sounding name.

Memory is so strange, I could never remember the accident when I was young, then one night forty years later I woke in the early hours and remembered every single thing about it. I was sweating and shaking when I woke, I could even remember the number plate on George's pickup truck FO 6571

The accident resulted in me having to spend sixteen weeks in hospital with all sorts of problems. When I came out, we had moved out of the house we shared, away from the dirty old man, into a flat near my Nana's, I think we had to move because of father's temper, Mr Wilkins was not prepared to put up with him any longer, it was very strange coming home to a strange house. There was no stair cupboard to hide in but there was a small shed in the back yard, this was used quite regularly.

So there we were living at the other end of town, Alexandra Road, the flat we lived in was in a large red-bricked Victorian house called Richmond, we were in a better part of town still poor but the area was cleaner and the sun shone a lot more. The flat had a back yard where I played with my sister, under protest, no garden so no more green leaf but the shed was a refuge from all the rows.

On the corner was Temple Lodge where Nana and Popa lived, they lived on the top floor, there were thirty-nine stairs up to the flat and I used to run up them trying to take as few steps as possible. I was always shouted at for making too much noise by the other tenants, but always called on by them to run errands and take messages.

Our new house was opposite the secondary modern school where I would eventually finish my education, a Victorian built school with two separate entrances, girls and boys, there was a cenotaph on the front lawn of the school with the names of past pupils who had lost their lives in the wars. Iron railings to keep people out surrounded the school but as kids we found a way in and used to play in the playground when school was finished.

In the flat above us lived a couple who had no children of their own so we got to call them Aunty and Uncle, Megan and Cyril Reynolds, they had a television and we were allowed to go up and watch children's television. This was a real treat. I remember the news about Ruth Ellis being hanged, watching the Coronation and the Suez Crisis, but I was more interested in the Lone Ranger and Tonto.

The flat was split level we had a bedroom kitchen and toilet on the ground floor, a bedroom and sitting room on the first floor, we had no bathroom, bath times were in the large Belfast sink in the kitchen. The kitchen was where we spent most of our time as it had an enclosed fire, this burned coke and used to smell when the wind was in the wrong direction, so we had it removed and a gas fire was installed in its place. We had lino on the floor and a rug by the fire, a kitchen table where meals were taken and two reasonably comfortable chairs for mother and father. There was also a radio and we listened to *The Archers* each night and *Lost In Space* at the weekends with Uncle Mac on Saturday. Our bedroom was directly above the kitchen on the first floor, we could hear the radio when we were in bed and we were lulled to sleep listening to the music.

Father had started a new job, he was now working for the cottage hospital, still as maintenance engineer but now earning ten pounds a week we were on the up, times were getting better. Mother could now smoke *Senior Service* instead of *Woodbines,* and we could have pocket money - three pence a week - a fortune.

But I missed Bouncing Bob's, no more treats, although there were bonuses, down the road from our new flat was the Ridgbourn. There were a few shops, a grocer, a tobacconist and sweet shop, a chip shop, owned by a nice old man called Alec Moorhouse, his wife was not very nice, she used to have ideas above her station, as my Nana used to say, but Alec, would always put a few extra chips in your bag, a piece of faggot and some batter bits. He always had a kind word and always asked after the family, he also had a small butchers shop, not very clean but no one died form Alec's meat. There was a sub Post Office which sold newspapers and a few toys to supplement the takings. The lady who owned the Post Office had very thick glasses and when she looked directly at you, her eyes seemed so big and scary, she never gave anything away. The sweet shop was heaven for us with all sorts of goodies, gob stoppers, sherbet dips, bubble gum, toffee. I would take a long time to spend three pence and the lady owner of the shop Mrs Dean, was not very patient with children and would tell us to hurry up, we never did.

The other direction from our flat took you to the local boating lake, this was reached by going up a steep hill, a nice place, there were ducks and swans on the lake we used to feed them bread. There were rowing boats, motorboats and canoes, this is where my love of rowing and boats stems from, I spent many hours rowing. It was also a favourite course fishing lake especially with people from Birmingham; it boasted huge carp of several varieties, also tench, chub, bream, perch and the occasional trout.

Alistair was my best friend in school, when Alistair and I were eleven years old we got into ‘a bit of trouble’ at the lake, no real damage was done it was just high spirits, but it was called ‘malicious damage’. We were criminals, outcasts and thugs.

We tried to get a boat into the water to row to the island in the middle of the lake, it sunk just like the Titanic, no orchestra playing but we whistled her demise into the murky depths, (all four feet of them). We were seen, and accused of breaking windows in the boathouse, we did not break any windows but as we were in the vicinity so we did it, because we sank the boat we got the blame for that as well.

The scorn we felt was terrible, we were eleven years old.

THIRTEEN AND SIX

We broke a window at the lake,
and pushed a boat into the water.
According to the rules of law,
we shouldn’t really oughta.
When hauled before the magistrates,
who treated us like dirt,
We stood proud before our lofty peers;
we both had on clean shirts.

‘Behaviour, such as you have shown,
will not be tolerated
We fine you, thirteen and six,
and place you on probation’.
A year apart we did agree,
on our word of honour.
But a year away from your best mate
wasn’t worth a dollar.

When the news hit the streets,
people they did frown,
Don't hang around with them
and never bring them home.
When we were old enough,
we both moved out of town,
We made our lives somewhere else
and never went back home.

Strange how times have changed, these days what we got up to would only get a telling off. Probably not even a fine, just a caution, how times have changed. We were worried we were told we would be sent to borstal, instead we were fined thirteen and sixpence each and put on probation for a year and had to report to a probation officer every Saturday morning. Nowadays the criminal feels unlucky if he serves five years for murder, even then he moans about his human rights!

Alistair, and I used to go fishing at the local river, the Ithon, we used to fish for trout, using worms as bait, so on the way to the river, we would call into the local sewerage works and dig for worms in the dry cesspool beds. These were the best worms in the world and almost guaranteed to catch a trout or two. Also at the sewerage beds tomatoes would grow in abundance. Of course they were never planted, but grew from the seeds that passed through the system so to speak, and grew wild, we would pick these tomatoes, and sell them to the local fruit and veg shop. I am not a great lover of tomatoes!

The boathouse also housed a café and ice cream parlour and at certain times of the year the lake area would be used to stage such events as the Welsh Three Day Motorcycle Trial, which is still held there but now has been reduced to two days. This was where my love of motorcycles came from. Above the lake up another steeper hill was the golf course, a links course, where the views were spectacular. Halfway up the golf course hill stands a small church The Old Parish Church where lots of my friends lie beneath the ground, looking out on the town they never left in life or death.

We were not too far from the Rock Park as it extended almost the whole length of the town and it was a short walk from the flat, so we visited the park regularly I was able to punch my Wellentonia tree. As I got older I found the need to punch my tree more frequent, probably frustration.

All in all the town was great, everything you wanted was there, the people were mostly friendly and you knew everybody, if you caused trouble you got your backside kicked and respect for other people was always observed. Everybody knew your family so it was foolish to think you could get away with anything. You were encouraged to hold doors open for ladies and to touch the peak of your cap to acknowledge people in the street. Manners were taught and strictly adhered to on pain of having a hiding if you were rude to anyone. What a pity those courtesies have been, to the greater part, let to slide.

Table manners were taught as part of your upbringing, no pudding unless dinner was finished. If you did not finish all your dinner then it was placed in front of you at tea and again at breakfast. You soon learned, to clear your plate, or try to encourage the dog under the table and feed your meal secretly to him when no one was looking.

If I ever did anything wrong Nana would always be the first to find out, she would say a little bird, she called the yellow tattler had told her, I never did catch that yellow tattler. I had lots of smacks and hidings, a part of growing up, I was no different to any other child of the working class, but I seemed to get more hidings than most. I can never remember looking forward to my father coming home, most kids I knew played with their father, I never did, he never had the time or patience so I kept out of his way as much as possible.

I once set the house on fire playing with a gas tap, which was fastened to the wall by the sink in the kitchen, this was used to connect, via a rubber hose, to a huge gas ring. On the gas ring a galvanised bath would be placed and filled with water to boil the washing, no washing machines then. One day when I was alone in the kitchen I got hold of a box of matches and, as kids do, started to play with them. I climbed up onto the kitchen worktop and turned on the gas tap, struck a match this in turn started a ferocious flame that I could not put out so I had to run upstairs to my father and tell him I had set the house on fire. I got a real hammering for that, I was seven years old.

I gave my sister a haircut, it seemed a good idea at the time, she had long ginger hair, mother had let it grow, she said it was beautiful, except when I had finished with it, this operation took place under the kitchen table with a pair of scissors taken from the sewing box. I was probably jealous of her hair, she never got smacked or told off for anything I had a real hammering for that. I seemed to go through life getting hammerings, I was getting used to them, sort of weekly medicine.

My first pet was a dog called Pal, he was a terrier of sorts, he slipped his lead and ran away and was killed by a car. A cat called Charlie replaced him. I can't remember what happened to him. Then came Mickey, a cocker spaniel, liver and tan with big floppy ears and a cold nose, he slobbered a lot but I did not mind, he was my best friend for the next ten years, we were inseparable. He followed me everywhere he would sit by me at meal times, knowing he would get fed, and jumped up on my bed to sleep, always slobbering, but he was my friend the best one I had for a lot of years.

I survived to the ripe old age of ten when we moved to a council house. We had been on the council list for five years, then all of a sudden we were given a brand new house in another part of town on Lant Avenue. This was a new extension to an old council estate, it was a nice house - number 38. Brand new, fresh paint smell, magnolia, every room the same colour, but it was bright and clean. We were the first people to live in it, somehow it made it very special, it had three bedrooms, a large sitting room with an open fire place, large kitchen and a dining room, with what was called a back to back oven and hob.

Just off the kitchen was the coalhouse and a large lean-to shed we called the washhouse, nobody ever washed in there, this was where Mickey, was to live in his box.

Upstairs there was a toilet and separate bathroom, I had never had a real bath, this was quite a thrill. I had my own bedroom overlooking fields, we had an attic which father had floor boarded with floorboards we nicked from the rest of the building site, he used to keep his tools and paint and other stuff we had no immediate use for, but did not want to throw away up there.

The garden was huge, front and back, there was easily enough room to build another two houses. We backed onto a farm and an old quarry, this quarry was to be my new playground and at the top of the quarry was a pool where I would spend a lot of time fishing and messing about. My friend Clive lived on the same estate so I had a friend there already.

My main job in the household was helping with the garden, which was vast. The work was very hard, builders had left what seemed like tons of broken bricks and concrete blocks, these had to be shifted to an old land fill site we called the dump, this was about a hundred yards down the road. Everybody used to dump garden waste and builders rubble there.

The garden had to be laid out so with every wheelbarrow of rubbish I took to the dump, I had to bring back a barrow load of topsoil, which the council had tipped there for this purpose, so my barrow was never empty. When the garden was dug and planted, guess what, more bloody green leaf. Laying out this garden involved many hours with the wheelbarrow and shovel. Life was getting harder, I was getting stronger, father did not scare me so much anymore, I had learned to duck and run.

I had three pets at this time, a three-legged cat called Sooty; she lost her leg in a confrontation with a mowing machine, although, it did not slow her down. A jackdaw, I rescued from the local boating lake, his name was Jack, he lived in a tea chest cage outside the back door. The cage would be open during the day and he would fly around but he always came back at night and of course Mickey, he was my constant companion, he slept in the shed, except when I sneaked him up to my bedroom, father was very hard on him.

Father being the eldest son of a gamekeeper considered Mickey a drain on the household budget, we should only have pets that could work. The cats caught mice but Mickey caught nothing, but Mickey was a pet and father never really came to terms with that, maybe, it was because he was my pet.

Other jobs involved sawing logs for the fire, this was to help stretch the coal out, I had to gather and drag home large logs from the farm with the aid of Mickey, he did not help but he kept me company.

Getting, the coal and logs for the fire was another task I did not particularly like, the coalhouse was very dark it had no light, so a torch was needed. Living in the coalhouse was the biggest spider I have ever seen, and despite my fears I never killed it. I think we reached an understanding, the spider would not attack me, I would not kill it, but it still frightened me. I still have a fear of spiders.

Life was hard and I was constantly dodging my father's slaps and punches. He kept telling me life is hard so I had better get used to it. He was not wrong.

SCUTTLING

Opening the coalhouse door, a scuttling was heard,
Not a very loud noise, but one to set your nerves,
I knew what was lurking, and entered with great fear,
That hairy, eight legged monster, scuttling so near.

A torch shaking in one hand, and shovel in the other,
Entering his domain, so dark and with a shudder,
Talking softly to myself, never showing fear,
Getting closer to the coal, into the darkness peer.

Then shovel in my shaking hand, a thrust into the coal,
The scuttling spider in the dark, was frightening my soul,
And then I saw him staring, from his stringy web,
Then all my nerves suddenly raced up to my head.

He watched me, motionless as I shovelled coal,
I'm sure that he was laughing, at my shaking soul,
He never did approach me, or give me any bite,
But I dreamed of that spider, sometimes in the night.

I was about to sit the eleven plus exam to determine which senior school I was to attend, there wasn't much time for study as I would get home from school and start work doing some job or other, I had been told to do that morning.

I would come home to an empty house, apart from my sister, mother and father would still be at work, so until their return we had to fend for ourselves. If my jobs were not done I got into trouble, so it was important to do my work before study, consequently I was usually too tired to study. A vicious circle was developing, work no study, study no work, I was in a catch 22 situation.

Whatever way I took I was going to be in the wrong, no work - row with father, no study - row with school, no result in eleven plus - shit from every direction.

There was no escape I was trapped in an ever-decreasing circle, one which I would have gladly jumped out of, had I known how.

Chapter Two
SCHOOLS

The first school I attended was, council run, Oxford Road Primary. Again Victorian in architecture and built in red brick, as were so many of the buildings in town, it was situated at the bottom of a very steep hill. It had very heavy doors and small windows, each pane of glass about six inches square, they opened like a fan from the top by means of chords, which were pulled. Not much air would get in through them, this resulted in smells lingering in the rooms, there were a lot of smells that lingered! Parquet blocks covered every floor. On the whole the school was comfortable and warm. It had a thick and sticky smell of body odour, urine and feet, the air had a sort of blue tinge that could almost be seen.

On entering the building you were faced with a long corridor which stretched the whole length of the school, this corridor was quarry tiled, red and gold, polished to a high gloss. This tiled floor extended into the cloakrooms off the corridor, all the classrooms were on one side and the assembly hall/gymnasium and cloakrooms on the other. Halfway up the corridor, high on the wall was the school clock, when you were in the top class you would be assigned to take it in turns to ring the bell for break time or home time. You had to go out of your class five minutes before and wait until the appointed hour, then ring the hand bell, the only problem with this was you missed the last five minutes of the lesson and if a story was being read you missed the last bit every time.

The classrooms were set out all the same except one for the first years, this was filled with very small seats and tables with boxes for toys and areas for play. All the other classrooms had wooden desks with flip up lids, where your books and pencils were kept, there were inkwells on the desk these were countersunk into the desk, to avoid spillage, ink was only used in the top class. The masters had the same sort of desk but much bigger. There would be works of art hanging on the classroom walls and pictures of Christ on the cross surrounded by disciples, hands clasped in prayer, along with other religious pictures, these were in every classroom, each had a different picture but always religious.

I did not enjoy school that much but I worked as hard as I could, I was suffering with my hearing so I missed quite a lot of what was going on until one teacher realised this and moved me to the front of the class so I could hear better, this did make a lot of difference and made the work a lot easier.

The staff, save one, were kind and helpful. There were five classrooms, starting from standard one and going to standard five, at standard five you were groomed for the eleven plus examination. This was where I first encountered John Ivor Jones. He was the only teacher who abused his power, he beat me, very badly, he was a man of great size, six feet tall, portly not quite fat, he wore thick round rim glasses and was slightly balding, he always wore a black suit with a fawn coloured cardigan, which had what looked like a gravy stain, under his jacket. Each night he would read a passage from *The Pilgrim's Progress* by John Bunyan, he was passionate about the bible and pilgrims progress in particular, he would grin all the time he was reading from it. His farewell to the class, 'beware of Beelzebub', to us ten-year-olds he was Beelzebub! He presented a formidable figure in front of ten-year-old children. He came from a small Welsh town called Llandovery, and would travel up on the train every Monday morning, the train was almost always late, he then lived in bed and breakfast digs for the week and travelled back home on Friday. He took the final year of junior school. In those days it was up to eleven plus standard. If you did something wrong in his class you would be punished, you had to be on your very best behaviour. Punishment was meted out with a rounders bat; this weapon was nine inches across and shaped like a tennis racquet, it was made of solid wood. He kept it in his desk, which he had padlocked in case anyone stole it. This bat was infamous, he had taught my mother and she remembered the first time he presented it to the class. He had poured red ink on this weapon, simulating blood of past victims, just to add to the fear. Theatricals such as this were entirely unnecessary. When he fetched this bat out, he would fondle it carefully, almost loving it, turning it around in his huge hands, stroking it as if it were a tactile sculpture crying out for his caress, sometimes pressing it to his lips, in love with this object of pain. He would position the recipient, give a last loving stroke to his bat, say 'touch your toes', then run at you and hit you as hard as he could. Just before he took the first step, he had a habit of clearing his throat of phlegm, as if building his strength. At the point of his phlegmish hoicke you would clench your teeth, close your eyes, grip your ankles and hope he was not going to hit you too hard, but he always hit hard. Most of those he hit would double in pain, cry, creep back to their desk and sob uncontrollably for what seemed like hours. John Ivor would then sit back at his desk shaking, very red faced, blow his nose in an off-white handkerchief wipe the snot off his face and continue the lesson, again clearing his throat of phlegm.

I had been hit before and took the punishment then, like the others, sobbed and got on with it, until one day he hit me so hard I fell forward with such force I hit my head on the stationary cupboard. I managed to get back to my desk which was near the classroom door, I can't remember what came over me as I pushed my desk over, spilling the ink and my books on the floor. I was projectile vomiting at the time and thinking what a mess I was in, I ran out of his class, shouting abuse and vomiting. I think I said 'bugger off John Ivor', I was in so much pain I don't know how I managed to run, but I did. I ran to my Nana's house. I was afraid to go home in case my father was there; he would probably have given me another hiding for running home. After cleaning me up, I was covered in vomit and tears, Nana went down to the school. She still had her hair in curlers and her headscarf on, under normal circumstances she would never be seen out of the house in her curlers, but if the headmaster, Mr Timothy, and another teacher, Billy Macintosh, aided by Miss Beard, the junior teacher and nurse, had not intervened, she would have killed him. She took the podger with her; this was a piece of broom handle about two feet long, used to stir the washing in the bathtub. She would have used it on him I am sure. I carried severe bruises for weeks after and an egg-sized lump on my forehead. No school for a week, I missed a lot of lessons but managed to catch up on most things, thanks to Billy Macintosh who delivered schoolwork to my house.

John Ivor only used this bat on the boys, although the punishment he inflicted on the girls in the class was just as bad. Without being physical, he degraded them in front of the whole class, he would make them show their underwear and stand on a stool whilst doing it, he would then walk around them poking fun at them. They would be in tears, sobbing and shaking with fear of this huge, dirty, old man. Some of the girls he degraded must still carry these memories with them today, what a memory to carry through life.

As far as I know, he was never reported to the authorities for any of his actions. In those days punishment that was handed out was never questioned, it was a normal aspect of life, "beat some sense into the child." Thank God, this has, for the greater part, changed. I still think that some form of mild punishment should be used in schools, as it is a way of enforcing the authority of the tutor, but not as John Ivor Jones dished it out.

Since that episode in my very young and vulnerable life, I have had a severe mistrust of anyone in authority. I remember this incident so clearly, it was a Tuesday and Tuesday was spelling day. My misdemeanour, I could not spell diphtheria. I wished that I had asked him what terrible thing happened to him when he was young to make him into such a sadistic person.

TEACHER

John Ivor Jones is a very bad man,
He goes to church on Sunday,
To pray to God, to give him strength,
To beat the kids on Monday.

The other teachers in junior school were kind. There was Billy Macintosh, he taught the year behind so he let me stay in his class after the beating, he told me if that man ever touches you again you come straight to me, he helped me get over the initial trauma although I never fully recovered from that beating. I never told my father about the incident, and made my nana promise not to tell him, mother knew but was told by Nana that the matter had been sorted out.

I worked hard to get through the eleven plus exam for grammar school. Despite all my best efforts I failed and went to a secondary modern. I blame the failure on the fact that I missed out on so much having to go back a class as I was terrified of John Ivor Jones. My father was the only one to hold this failure against me, as he did on many future occasions. The reason for his disappointment had something to do with a cousin, the Boy David I called him, or *Little Lord Faulteroy*, as my mother referred to him. My father's parents had bought David up and he had got into grammar school, having passed the eleven plus, which made my father feel that I was less than adequate. He need not have felt that way, I was feeling pretty inadequate myself.

Secondary School

Secondary school was pretty good I was reasonably clever, which did help, as I didn't have to work so hard to stay near the top of the class. I did feel disappointed at my failure but decided it was best to draw a line under it and get on with whatever was coming.

The first experience of pain at secondary school was the dentist. The school dentist used to come once a year. He used to turn up in a white caravan converted into a torture chamber, smelling of disinfectant and gas.

The big black chair, the tray, full of weird looking tools made to inflict, pain, the finger thrust into your mouth and the words; 'open wide, this won't hurt a bit'. Lying bastard, it did hurt - it hurt like hell. The waiting - sitting at your desk, trying not to think of it, then your name would be called and your heart would miss several beats, you would stagger from your seat, trying not to look terrified in front of your classmates. Gasping for breath, trying to stop your knees from shaking, you would make your way to the chamber of pain, thinking all the time, shall I run home, but knowing, if you did all your mates would call you coward, but what you did not think of was they were all thinking the same thing, when their turn came.

As I entered the chamber I looked around at the array of instruments and posters on the wall, which told tales of terrible problems if you did not clean your teeth, the deformed and raw looking gums. These were enough to scare the pants off me.

The chair and the dreaded gas bottles, the rubber mask, a thought flashed through my mind, would he gas me? or would I have that three foot needle thrust into my mouth, almost reaching to my toes, and the numbing feeling as my whole mouth deadened. All the time looking to see what instrument would he pick up, would it be the pliers, or would it be the drill? The drill used to grind and the sensation and vibration would shake my whole body and I would grip the sides of the chair, almost pulling the arms off. All the time the masochistic bastard would be saying, "not long now," the lying toe rag, it used to take hours, then the rinse, that foul tasting pink liquid, and I would try to spit but my mouth was dead and I missed the little white swirling, sucking, gurgling sink, then I was swiftly, pushed back into the chair and again the finger would be in my gob, and he would start again.

Then would come the filling, it felt just like someone was dragging something hard, against my teeth, then 'ok rinse out' I'd spit again and again, miss the sink, then he would say 'ok all done', and I'd be out of that seat, so fast in case he changed his mind, and had another go.

If, you had to have a tooth out, he would gas you, the mask would be slowly bought to your terrified face and he would repeat, over and over again, breathe deeply. The smell, used to make you feel like throwing up, then nothing. The next thing you knew you were vomiting, violently into the sink and he would be saying, 'all done just relax'. Jesus, he had just taken out one of your teeth, you were sick to your stomach, and terrified and this arsehole, was telling you to relax! Where were these people coming from.

No wonder I still have a great fear of dentists. When I was seventeen, I had an accident and damaged, my front teeth, instead of capping them, a dentist, named Tweeny, took four of my front teeth out, and one at the back. The back tooth was perfectly all right, but he needed an anchor point to hold the new false teeth in place. If I had one wish it would be to have my own teeth again, these false ones look very nice, but they give me some terrible headaches. Bloody dentists. When I have dental treatment now. I have to have general anaesthetic. If I am not unconscious I tell them I will not be responsible for my actions, I don't think I will ever get over my fear of the tooth doctors.

Pain is a strange thing, it's surprising how soon a toothache goes when you are waiting in a dentist's waiting room. The agony you go through making the decision, to go and when you get there, the pain doesn't seem so bad, must be physiological, or is it the fear of the cure is worse than the ailment?

Whatever it is, you eventually have to get the tooth sorted out and after it is done, you wonder what all the fuss was about, but it still does not help to get you there.

TEETH

This won't hurt, you hear them say, as you sit upon the chair.
Don't worry now please relax, you're not going anywhere.
Now open wide this, won't take long, we haven't got all day.

I'll have a good look at them, and then I'll have my say.
The prodding of the instrument, the scraping on your teeth,
His assistant stands beside him, taking notes as he speaks.
He talks to you and questions, as you stare into the sky,
The reflection of your frozen face, clearly in his eyes.
Rinse your mouth he orders, and we'll see what can be done,
I think you need some fillings and we need to check your gums.
How often do you clean your teeth, and tell me do you floss?
I think that the hygienist, is going to want to look.
Tell me what's your preference, needle or the gas,
It will not hurt the treatment, and the pain it will soon pass.
You know that they are lying, but you trust them to do their best,
Just fix the tooth that's aching, and please don't touch the rest.
At last you get up off the chair, and pay him for his skill,
And as you walk out through the door, you pop a couple of pills.
The numbness soon wears off, and then you feel no pain,
But brush them well every day, or you'll be back again.

The school again Victorian in it construction was a two storey building and housed on average three hundred and fifty pupils and thirteen staff. The ground floor was comprised of the assembly hall and gym, cloakrooms, the maths, geography, domestic science and one of the two English rooms. The corridor was L shaped, two flights of stairs next to the geography room took you up to the art room, the other English room, which also doubled as the religious instruction room, the library, science lab, music room, the administration and headmaster's room.

In the playground were two prefabricated buildings, wooden huts, these housed the history room and yet another English and religious instruction room. Across the yard was a separate brick building, which was the woodwork and metal workshop, behind that block was the canteen.

The playing fields were reached by taking a run through the Rock park, this was a run of about two miles. I only managed to get there once or twice, I used to disappear with a couple of others and either go fishing or go back to the school library.

I had few friends when I was in school, I don't socialise well, I feel inadequate in a lot of ways. My hearing is not so good so I tend not to hear what people say, I don't converse well due to this, I have a perforated eardrum this was caused by being hit on the head so much when I was young. I have been told I have selective hearing, this is not the case, if I am not looking at the person who is speaking I sometimes mis-hear, I can't lip read but it does help if I can see who is talking.

Secondary school was very different to what I had been used too, there was such a mix of people. Neville Evans, the woodwork master, not a very big man slightly balding who always wore a white work coat with several pencils and an expanding ruler stuffed into the top pocket, along with his pipe when it wasn't in his mouth. He was out of his tree, (clever pun eh?) he talked endlessly about wood and the war, he served in the RAF and always made a big thing of this fact. 'If I had you lot in the RAF I would lick you into shape by God I would', this was one of his favourite sayings. He used to tell us he cooked eggs on the wings of his spitfire in the Sahara desert. Where the hell did he get eggs from in the middle of the dessert? I never asked him that. He told so many stories about the war, me being somewhat of a sceptic left the first class I attended ducking for cover. I was a bit of an exhibitionist, this seemed to annoy him, so consequently every class I attended after that first introduction I was ducking for cover. He seemed to take an instant dislike to me, I wonder why? He would chuck lumps of his precious wood at me and all the time his false teeth were clenching his pipe, belching thick shag smoke like the exhaust of his spitfire. It was a horrible sight. The spit would run down the stem of his pipe and dribble onto his jacket in big brown blobs only to be wiped away leaving the stain as evidence. He did let me have a go on his precious lathe once. I was trying to make a fruit bowl, but the chisel I was using jarred from my hand. I was so nervous he was standing next to me supervising my every movement, this was as close as he'd ever stood to me, without trying to choke me. The smell of his *St Julian* tobacco was strong and choking, his smoke was swirling around my head and up my nose. The chisel took his pipe out of his mouth, he went mad, it was time to run. He told me repeatedly, I was not a patch on my old man. BIG DEAL!

The reason for this comment was that, when the war was over, my father who had served in the Royal Navy had attended night classes in carpentry and cabinet making, a sort of rehabilitation course. Guess who took those classes? Yes it was the pipe-smoking ace of WW2.

As the school years passed he did seem to warm to me slightly and there were times I thought he really liked me. I always made sure I was smartly dressed in school my shoes were always clean, my hair cut and my tie was always straight except when he tried to strangle me with it, this seemed to impress him. When I left school he would come into the butcher's shop where I was working and chat to me about all sorts of subjects, almost treating me as a long lost friend, what strange people these teachers were.

The other nutter in secondary school was the art teacher, David Jenkins. I couldn't even trace a drawing, let alone paint a picture, I still can't, but I could get right up his nose.

This man was huge, his hands were enormous and his shoulders just fit through the door of his classroom. He had a mop of curly, grey-ginger hair, he always wore a Harris tweed jacket that was never buttoned with pens and pencils stuffed into the top breast pocket. He never walked, he strode, his fists would be clenched tightly by his side, slowly keeping time with his legs as he walked. When you passed him in a corridor it was a natural instinct to duck as he came up to you, sometimes his fist would lash out, if he caught you it would sting, if he didn't he would remember, and try and get you next time. We called him the Necker.

He had an ongoing affair with the domestic science teacher Miss George. I don't think it ever got past the flirting stage, but they were always in a huddle when the opportunity presented itself. Miss George took domestic science and personal hygiene. God she was ugly, she would turn milk sour by just glancing at it, she was always checking my fingernails, probably because I always kept them clean and short and she thought it was not normal to have short clean nails if you were a schoolboy. She never commented on my nails but would always check them whenever she saw me, a fetish maybe? The Necker saw something in her, maybe it was her mind, there was nothing else. Maybe she was checking his nails as well.

He was a real nutter; he would hit you from one end of the classroom to the other, then pick you up and start again.When the class first met him, his opening gambit was.

"It will remain to be seen how many of you will please me and how many will incur my wrath and temper, which is not a pretty sight."

This statement was, made with, rolling eyes and clenched fists.

He was an accomplished potholer and took part in many underground rescues. He was a very good pot thrower too, both in the sense he would chuck one at you, and he could make one. All feared him, pupils and staff alike. Although he was a mad so and so in school, when he was in Civvy Street so to speak he was a really nice man, but God help you if he ever saw you up to mischief out of school he would make you pay when he got you in school.

I must have had an aura around me that said come and hit me I don't mind, well I did mind, I minded a lot. It was hard enough dodging my father at home without having to put up with the same treatment in school, so I made a stand. The next time I was hit, I told the Necker that was the last time he would ever lay hands on me. My famous speech was. 'You are getting older, I am getting stronger and I have a long memory'.

I was never beaten again, at least not in school.

NECKER

We used to call him Necker, this giant of a man
He walked like a gorilla, and had full twelve inch hands
He was our art master, this creature who spelt fear
But when you got to know him, he really was a dear.

There were tutors I did get on with like my English teachers. There were three of them and I got glowing reports from all, mostly for my wild imagination and story telling. Composition was my favourite subject, I have always had a wild imagination. I was also good at science, geography and my favourite subject - history.

My first English teacher, Mrs Jones, was a lady from the tip of her head to her toes. She was aged about forty, quite old to us then but a very attractive lady. She always dressed to perfection, never a hair out of place, she had a few of us boys drooling on more than one occasion. We always knew when she had walked by, the smell of her perfume would linger and we all slowed down so we got the full benefit of this fragrance. She always wore flowing dresses, which swirled as she walked, sending the fragrance of her perfume wafting through the school. She was so gentle and loved reading to the class, she never sat behind her desk, there were no barriers between her and the class, all the boys were in love with her, I was no exception. She would encourage us all to read anything we could get hold of, someone once mentioned *Lady Chatterley's Lover*. She smiled and said if you can get a spare copy I would be interested in it, we all laughed at this comment as it was a banned publication at that time. We were encouraged, not forced, and we were all very upset when she left, none of us knew why she left but we found out she had died very suddenly of cancer. She worked almost up to the day she died, I missed her, she was a great help and befriended a lot of pupils, I wish I could remember the smell of her perfume. She was one of a different type of teacher, they would gently take you through a lesson there was no threat, not like the Necker and Neville the wood.

Brothers, John and Stanley Watkins, were the only teachers who wore cap and gown, this impressed me and I had visions of having a cap and gown of my own one day, alas a pipe dream. John taught English, we used to kick up a fuss in his class but we never meant any harm, he once marched all the boys in his class, myself included, to the headmaster's office and demanded he cane us for unruly behaviour. He was well within his rights, we did give him a hard time, we all lined up outside the head's office and one by one, were summoned in for the cane. The headmaster, Ken Vaughn, was a strict but very fair man. When I was in the fourth form he confiscated ten *Park Drive* cigarettes and a lighter I had in my pocket, but the day I left school I was summoned into his office and he gave them back to me. I couldn't smoke them as they had dried out so much the tobacco just fell out of the end of the paper tube, the lighter did not work either he had been using it.

The punishment was administered by means of a bamboo cane, this was struck across the palm of your hand and this did sting. The master, John Watkins was waiting outside the office with tears coming down his cheeks and he was apologising to us, we never played him up again, and he was treated by our class with the greatest of respect, and consequently he taught us well. John also took a class in gardening, a strange subject but we all enjoyed it.

Stanley, John's brother, older by a couple of years, taught Geography. He was different to John, in as much as you did not ever kick up a fuss in his class he was very strict. His lessons were not always about geography, he would tell tales of his days at university, life during the war years and his childhood, which was very hard. He was fascinating, he would stroll up and down the rows of desks and whisper to you if you were not doing so well, 'there, there my boy there, there'.

During the evenings both brothers could be found in the reading room of the local library, they were creatures of habit. Alistair and I would be hiding in the bandstand near the library having a smoke, and at five every evening they would go into the reading room and at seven-thirty they would leave.

John and Stanley lived in the same house with a sister and another brother, but they always travelled to school separately, John had a Morris Minor traveller and Stanley had a Volkswagen beetle. They never married, pity the line stopped with them. When I left school I was allowed to call them by their Christian names, but I always, attached Mister before addressing them, out of respect I suppose.

A master, who was very supportive of my efforts, was an author, he wrote under a pseudonym but I can't remember what it was, he taught English to the more senior classes up to G.C.E. level, he also taught religious instruction. Harry Fletcher, he actually grew up in the same village, Amroth in Pembrokeshire, as my Nana, (the Greek) more of her later, they were very good friends. He was a very gentle man, he never raised his voice, or criticised work unduly, He drove an old 1955 Bentley, and if he had a spare lesson, he would gather up any waifs or strays (those who should have been studying but were skiving), and take us all into an old part of the school gymnasium where he had accumulated several old engines, there he would teach us practical mechanics, he had such enthusiasm. He always wore his reading glasses even when he was driving they would be perched on the end of his nose which made him look as if he was squinting.

Then there was Denver James, he gave more to me than I realised, he taught Maths. I was useless at Maths, he gave me a hell of a time in his class, he used to keep me in at break times and try his best to get the meaning of numbers and angles into my head, but to no avail. I was so thick when it came to maths he used to throw his arms up in the air and give up, but Denver had a love of poetry and choral speaking, and at this I did excel. I could act the part I was reading, and make up a rhyme about almost anything at a moment's notice and as such, he inspired me to write. He always said I would go as far as the end of the road with maths. He was not wrong. When I left school I called him Denver sir. I built up quite a relationship with all my ex teachers, I always respected them. As the years went by, I realised how difficult a job they had to do. Therefore, I am glad to say, I made my peace with all but one. John Ivor Jones, he had died a few years previously, I had always intended to get in contact with him and try to make my peace, sort of lay the ghost, but alas it was too late. Pity.

School days were reasonably uneventful academically, I seemed to be able to get a good mark without really trying too hard and consequently, drifted along with the tide, gaining some recognition from my peers and being able to keep my low profile (cool eh?).

I was always getting spotted doing something that was against some rule or other, consequently I did not aspire to any great heights. I was never made a prefect or given any responsibility, this I know disappointed my mother, but I never wanted to have any responsibility over others, I was happy to drift along with the tide.

I won the school first prize for composition, the prize, a book, *Tales Of The Wild West*, by Max Brand. It was a crap read, but I treasured that book for years, it was the only prize I ever won. I tried sports, but did not excel, I particularly hated football and still do to this day.

I used to skive off to my Nana's for a smoke and a cup of tea. Nana never discouraged my smoking, so Alistair and I used to skive a lot to Nana's especially when the lesson was games or PE.

Our games master was a brutal pig who used to get a great deal of pleasure out of other's pain, although he never inflicted any on me. Lyn Jones was his name, again out of school he was a really nice man, I wonder was it some kind of a switch that was activated when these teachers passed through the school gates that turned them into brutal idiots. His only redeeming feature was that his second subject was history. He always took time over his history lessons and on the whole they were very good and my interest in history stemmed from his tutelage, especially the First World War, which I have carried on into adulthood, I still find this subject fascinating.

Each year the school held its Eisteddfod, this was a competition between three houses, and these were named after the three rivers that were in the vicinity of the town, Ithon, Wye and Edw. Everyone was expected to do their bit to help their house win the school shield. The competitions were many and varied; music, art, woodwork, choral, speaking, choir singing, folk and modern dance and sport.

I enjoyed the school Eisteddfod, particularly the choral speaking and poetry, my 'non-de-plume' was Pedro, I was in Ithon house. Denver was the master in charge of Ithon house and as such, expected each of us to give our all, in order to win the Eisteddfod shield, this we did, we won more times than we lost. I met Denver just by chance twenty years after leaving Llandrindod Wells, he remembered me instantly, what a man.

Choral speaking gave me the start I needed to write, not poetry but rhymes, that have a meaning to me because many are based on true stories, and I believe that anything that happens in your life, be it funny or tragic, should be recorded for your family.

Many people have no idea what their history is.

I did win one more prize in school it was a dance competition for the cha-cha-cha with that cuddly girl called Norma. Norma was a very down-to-earth girl, she called a spade a spade but she was well respected. She had short dark brown hair and grey eyes that could flash at you and stick you in their gaze, making you feel elated or ashamed, she flashed them a lot when we danced. I made a lot of wrong moves but she was a great laugh and a very good dancer. I will never forget Norma; she led me a merry dance. She hounded me into the cha, cha, so I had to give in or she threatened to beat me up!

FOR NORMA

Norma was a cuddly girl
She could dance a sexy whirl
To dance with her gave such a thrill
Better than a pep-up pill
We won a prize Norma and me
The cha, cha, cha, we danced so sweet
To win a prize it was a treat
But never again we did meet
Oh what a girl was Norma

My first kiss was when I was eleven years old. I was a slow starter, the first girl I ever had a crush on was Sandra Evans, she had long auburn hair and the prettiest face, but she was not my first kiss, despite all my efforts, all the sweets and a night at the pictures, I still didn't manage to kiss her. My first kiss was with a girl who in later life tried to kill me, she ran into me while I was on my motorbike. She was driving a Triumph Herald and crashed right into my motorbike, a 250cc Royal Enfield. If she had wanted to kiss me again that much, she only had to ask there was no point, in trying to kill me! I will always regret not kissing Sandra but maybe it was not meant to be.

Oh! The first one, her name was Carroll, very blond hair, deep blue eyes but a snobbish attitude, her father owned a large garage and I think she thought she was better than most. When I met her years later she had changed into a real snob.

When I was in school girls took a back seat, I had no interest in them, well not much. There was a girl, her name was Elizabeth Ross, Sandra had taken to ignoring me, she had her eye on someone else a few classes above, she had her hair cut, I can't think why, she had beautiful hair down to her waist. Elizabeth had been fostered by a local family, her adopted father was a Major in the army and was in charge of the local army cadet force, so I joined the cadets to gain some points.

Elizabeth, had long, jet-black silky hair, eyes so brown you disappeared into them, and skin soft and olive brown. She was Asian, a very beautiful girl, I was desperately in love with her and I think she had some feelings for me. We would meet in town and just sit and talk, we thought a lot of each other and shared many secrets and fears. She disappeared one day and never came to school again, I am sure she had been promised to someone, but I don't suppose I will ever know. I did suffer some heartache after Elizabeth disappeared. I gave up the army cadets.

When you were young, your parents always told you that school days were the best days of your life, how long was it until you realised that they were telling lies? Ok in school you had no responsibilities, no wages to earn, all you meals provided, a roof over your head and clothes on your back. You were given pocket money and taken on holiday, that is if you were lucky, if not school was a drag. You were pressured in all subjects, homework was a drag, you had to work after school to make pocket money and holidays were none existent. You had to work at home because your parents were constantly at work, trying to make ends meet, and you had to cook your own meals, then to top it all, the roof over your head leaked. When you look around, today's children have things much the same, so things have not changed that much. Life goes on in much the same way, wages are still low, hours are long, pressure is horrendous, parents still have to work long hours trying to make ends meet, the cost of living goes up daily. So do you find yourself saying to your children that school days are the best years of your life?

School holidays would find me working for most of the time but there were times when I could join in with all the kids in the street. We would play cricket or tennis, we made trolleys, or as some called them go-karts, out of old pram wheels, and go camping with nothing more than a tin of beans and some bread.

Fishing was another pastime, the taste of fresh fried fish cooked over an open fire by the riverbank is a taste I will always remember. We made bows and arrows, played cowboys and Indians and built dens to hide in.

Girls were as bad as the boys, joining in with whatever game or adventure was ongoing on the day. There would be so much to do in the summer, the six weeks holiday seemed to pass so quickly.

The highlight of the year was bonfire night. For months we would collect and store paper, boxes, tyres, anything that would burn. A month before the 5th, we would begin to build the bonfire starting with the centre pole and building a frame covering it all around with branches, always making a den inside, the format was never changed, the finished construction was some twenty feet high and big enough inside to house two family cars, this was eventually filled with all the collected fuel.

On the night, a party would be held for the whole street

arranged by the parents. There were not many fireworks but the party and the fire, were more than enough to make up for it. We would have baked potatoes, sausages and meat cooked on a barbecue, soft drinks for the kids and beer for the adults, except the ladies who would usually have shandy or cider. We had the usual bonfire raids, this was when other streets raided each other's bonfire to try and pull it down, but it was mostly good-natured fun.

In our street lived Donald Mason who had diabetes, he was always happy and smiling, he never complained or cried, he was so strong. Sadly Donny died of diabetes, another waste, he was a happy person and no problem to anybody. His mum, dad and sister were devastated

PLAYMATES

Wouldn't it be nice today if kids could only learn to play?
Instead of causing so much grief,
learn to play and keep the peace.
With hopscotch and the skipping rope,
the tennis ball and cricket bat.
Football matches no one won,
the games we played were so much fun.
No problems then the kids would cause,
for drinks of pop we'd take a pause,
And sweets were always shared around
except for Donny he wasn't allowed.
Diabetes was his ill,
but apples and pears he ate his fill,
We always helped each other out
and some of the time we all fell out.
But when a game was in full swing
everybody would join in.
Wouldn't it be nice today,
if kids could only learn to play?

In the summer evenings, as we got older short trousers turned into jeans, the games in the street were forgotten, time for more excitement. We used to hang around town, being a nuisance, I was no exception. The evenings were traditional, boys from all over town would congregate and tell tales and smoke woodbine cigarettes, most of us were violently sick the first time we smoked, but we carried on regardless.

The main street in Llandrindod Wells was flanked by two lanes, Tudor Lane was on the east side, this was a rough lane full of potholes and a particularly nasty corner, the local slaughterhouse was in Tudor Lane this is where I served my apprenticeship.

The west side was Middleton Lane, here we could sometimes steal a bottle of sparkling wine from the rear of the Glen Usk Hotel, it was terrible stuff but with a woodbine or two it wasn't so bad and we felt very grown up.

In order to get from one lane to the other, you had to cross the main road Middleton Street at either end. We would race around the lanes on bicycles and across the street, it was quite dangerous as we almost collided with cars. There were a few nasty spills and lots of cuts and grazes it was great fun especially when it was dark.

The local police sergeant, Wilfred Earnest Gorman, six feet six inches tall in his socks, was after us. He was tenacious, he'd chase us all over town but never managed to catch us in the act of any mischief. Someone would always be keeping watch for Sergeant Gorman and when he was spotted the cry 'cops' would ring out and everybody would scatter in different directions. He would always shout after us; 'I know who you are, I'll see your fathers', but he never did, he got us all in his own time one by one. I will never forget when he got me.

A challenge. Half a crown was collected and whoever knocked the sergeant's hat off his head, got the money. In the sixties the police in Llandrindod wore flat caps, no helmets at that time. So you would need to get very close to him to do this dastardly deed, half a crown was enough to buy a packet of fags and a night at the pictures, this was serious money. So a dateline was set, the deed had to be done before a certain date, or the money would be divided up again each having his stake back. I managed to do the deed after days of plucking up the courage and picking my time and place. I rode my bike so fast down the street after spotting him and with my heart in my mouth reached out and knocked his hat clean off his head, I was surprise how far a flat cap could roll and it was overtaking me but I dare not look around at the sergeant for fear of being recognised. To my surprise, the sergeant did not call my name, but he did yell after me, I was safe or so I thought. My heart was in my mouth, all the way home that night, I expected to see him standing at the door with my father, I certainly expected a hammering, but nothing. I was a hero.

A couple of weeks went by, and I was still feeling elated at my heroic task, then one night when cycling to my evening job, which was cleaning up the local slaughterhouse, I came across the sergeant, 'hello young Roberts', he greeted me, 'come and look what I've just found'. As I got off my bike he gave me such a clip on my ear I saw stars. When I went home that night my father asked if there was anything I wanted to tell him, I said no, then he asked why my ear was so red so I told him, then I got a slap on the other ear, to match them up, he said, 'that's for knocking Wilf's hat off'.

I don't think either clip on the ear did me much harm, anyway it got me half a crown and the respect of my mates. It may be a good thing to let the police have a more hands on approach to minor problems that seem to be plaguing our society today.

A FRIENDLY CLIP

The policeman used to be the man,
we could respect and trust,
We always counted on him,
in times of need and must.
He used to clip you round the ear,
if trouble you did cause,

Then if you thought of going wrong,
you'd stop and think and pause.
The days of that are sadly gone,
of this we are quite sure,
The policeman gets no respect,
not like the days of yore.
But who's the first man on the scene,
when problems reappear,
We all shout for the policeman
to suddenly appear.
So spare a moment for the cop,
and help him when you can,
You may be in need of him one day
to lend a helping hand.

~*~

I left school at sixteen after GCSE exams, I did intend joining the Royal Navy but memories of John Ivor Jones were still locked into my mind and the thought of being bullied put the mockers on that plan.

There were a succession of girlfriends, one night stands as we called them, and I don't mean that in a bad way, there were a few steady girls, but my interest at that time were more on motorcycles than girls, but I do remember them all, we had a lot of fun and a few broken hearts. I always expected to bump into Norma at one of the Saturday night discos but never did, I never saw Norma again. Many years later, I learned she became a nurse and had moved away. Pity I would have liked to have met her out of the school environment.

I used to fall in love every other week I think everybody does at that age, I can still feel the heartache of the break-ups even now. It's a strange feeling like someone is stirring your stomach, very slowly, with a big spoon, you find it hard to breathe and your heart feels like it's going to explode, you can't concentrate or eat, your sleep is permanently interrupted and you're always late for work, for which you receive many warnings and are threatened with the sack. Then you fall in love again and the whole process starts over and it's worse than the last time.

Then there are the songs, you always remember the songs, wherever you go in your life if that song starts to play, your mind goes back to the particular love you had at that time. Jim Reeves sang a song called *Distant Drums (Mary, Marry Me)*, this always brings back a memory or two.

There is no escape, everyone goes through it, unless you are a Trappist monk or a hermit, but who's to say it wasn't love that drove them to their calling? Or it may be that they dodged cupid's arrows on purpose, knowing what was to come.

I still have a burning ambition to kiss Sandra, and I think this will always be with me, she was the elusive butterfly.

School days over.

Chapter Three
FAMILY

Grandfather Roberts

Builth Wells in Breconshire, a small market town on the banks of the River Wye, a pretty town with a large park where the annual May Fair would come and the town came to life. Hundreds of people from surrounding areas would come for the shows. Nowadays the Royal Welsh Agricultural Show moves into town and the town takes on the appearance of the Klondike in the gold rush days.

The locals on the whole are old-fashioned people, not used to change, although at the same time craving for more amenities. The town has a cinema, an arts centre, and cricket, football and rugby are well catered for as well as a reasonable golf course. It has a country club for the more well off and a community centre for those who are not so well off. It is a friendly town for the most part but a rivalry between Llandrindod Wells and Builth Wells and Rhayader has always been much in evidence, especially at the local dances.

The town was built beside the River Wye, a famous salmon river in its day, a very beautiful river wide, fast flowing, clean, very popular with canoeists and ramblers. This was where my father's father was a gamekeeper. He was a Hampshire man, after the 1914/18 War he moved from Hampshire to take up the position of junior gamekeeper at the Caer Beris estate, then later as head gamekeeper.

Caer Beris, was owned by Lord Swansea, John Hussey Hamilton Vivian, who farmed the 11,000 acre estate. He succeeded his father at the age of nine, he was educated at Eton and was one of the greatest marksmen of his day, he served as chairman of the British Shooting Sports Council. Caer Beris regularly held shoots and my grandfather being head gamekeeper had his work cut out preparing for these events. Catering for the nobility was a very demanding job and much care had to be taken to ensure no shooter was accidentally injured and at the same time making sure everybody had a good day's sport. Caer Beris is on the banks of the River Irfon, it joins the Wye about six miles lower than the point the River Ithon joins, this causes the Wye to grow bigger and stronger forging its way to the River Severn joining the Severn Estuary at Chepstow.

My grandfather, Tom Roberts, came from Overton in Hampshire and was a very hard working man, although he never talked to me that much. I have many relatives in Builth, I don't know any of them that well, living in Llandrindod we were considered better than we ought to be, so communication was kept to the barest minimum.

Granddad, as we called him, was a very practical man, he made fishing lures, wooden whistles, walking sticks and he also made his own cartridges for shooting. He grew vegetables for the table, the best runner beans I have ever tasted, best eaten raw straight from the vine, crunchy and sweet. Flowers were grown for bulbs or blooms to sell. He also kept a pig for curing into ham and bacon. Amongst his other interests he repaired guns and gave fishing and shooting lessons to the many guests at Caer Beris. If you were lucky he would forecast the year's weather for you with a little saying. *If the Oak comes out before the Ash, we'll only have a little splash. If the Ash comes out before the Oak, we're bound to have a bloody soak.*

He was a hard man, well used to what life had to throw at him, and he did his share of throwing things back at life, he was swift with the stick and slow with the hugs. He never showed any affection for his family, although in his stone-like heart he surely felt something but never weakened enough to show it. In his later years when we would visit he would look up from his chair and say, "Well what brings you here? I bet you've been up to some mischief and devilment." He was a very clever, but a vicious man. He had seen sights and witnessed horrors that would give him nightmares all his life; he had served with the Hampshire Regiment on the Somme during the Great War. He never spoke of it and I was repeatedly told not to ask questions about it, although I was desperate to know what it was like, I never had the courage to ask. I should imagine he had been greatly affected by his time spent in the trenches. The war must have altered his state of mind. He was stern and tough, he was only a little man, no more than five feet four inches tall though his power was tremendous and he ruled the household with a fist of iron.

He and grandmother had eight children; Mary, Raymond, Alan, Leonard, Glyn, Vera, Olive and Martin, who were all born on the Caer Beris estate, at the tied house called The Pheasantry.

Granddad was very well respected and knew his stretch of the river well, he would patrol it watching for poachers which were in abundance during the hours of darkness from October to the end of November, they would be after the salmon with gaff and torch. He spent many nights crouched low behind some bush or other trying to catch them, he had a sawn off four-ten shotgun fashioned into a pistol, which he carried everywhere he went, he was not afraid to use it.

Caer Beris estate skirted the river so he would be constantly looking for those who would shoot the pheasants and other game. He looked after the shoots and breed the pheasants for the nobility to shoot. He was a countryman in every sense. He relied on only one person apart from himself, that was the Lord of the Manor who employed him, but more often than not he would tell the Lord who was a deal younger than him, how to proceed in order to get the most from the estate.

He was not a religious man he could never see the spiritual side of anything but he must have prayed during his life having gone through the experiences he had.

He had his own string of Labrador dogs that were kept in kennels and were often treated better than he treated his family. He would never hit a dog, instead if a dog was not behaving he would call it to one side and bite its ear, the dog usually behaved after that. All he needed were the tools of his trade, his guns, fishing rods and a sharp knife.

THE GAMEKEEPER

Don't be afraid of granddad, my Granny used to say,
He had it rough when he was young, it's just his silly ways.
He tries to love all you kids, but finds it very hard,
So when he comes home for his tea, please play out in the yard.

If he shouts and yells at you, try to understand,
The job he has is very hard, his work makes big demands.
His boss he is a Lord you see, and owns a big estate,
Our home and life depend on him, I know it's hard to take.

So when Granddad comes down the path, gun under his arm,
I try to smile, but it's no good, I feel I have to run.
I'd like to ask him questions, but I'm told it's never done,
About his job I'd like to know, and look at that big gun.

A gamekeeper I should have been, gun under my arm,
Looking after great estates and walking over farms.
Checking all the wildlife and organising shoots,
Turn out like Granddad? No thanks, they're not my roots.

Granddad was very hard to understand. He was a countryman and as such used to country ways and isolation. He could be found most Saturday afternoons on his one afternoon off work, he worked six and a half days a week, watching the cricket, or gardening, I have hankered after such isolation from time to time.

When I was about eight or nine I was visiting for a couple of days, this was a rare occasion as I lived in Llandrindod, seven miles away. I can't remember why I was deposited on them, I know it wasn't by choice. I do remember sleeping in a very cold and unwelcoming room. What I particularly disliked was the toilet, it was at the top of the garden, a none flushing type, the seat was two planks of wood joined together with a hole cut out and a large bucket underneath, it was horrible. The spiders were as big as the one in our coalhouse at home and the smell was not at all inviting. Newspapers were cut into squares threaded onto hairy string and hung on the door, this had a spy hole in the shape of a heart, one would balance on the plank seat and try and get the business done as soon as possible, it was a good exercise in finding out how long you could hold your breath. At night if we needed to go there would be a chamber pot under the bed, it was terrible and I hated it. I had only ever used a flushing toilet, I had been spoilt.

Granny Jessie

My grandmother, Jessie, was a wonderful woman; five feet tall and trim, so kind and sweet, always smiling despite the very hard life she endured.

She came from Dorston in Herefordshire, I never saw her without her apron on, it was a wrap around type and she was continually wiping her hands on it. She had been in service before she married she was an accomplished worker in all housework chores.

She never complained or raised her voice; despite having to put up with very primitive conditions. Her kitchen was always warm and welcoming, the range was always gleaming and there was fresh bread and cakes always on the go. She worked very hard, bringing up eight children of her own and in later life bringing up a cousin who was born out of wedlock. I had a very soft spot for her but again she never showed much affection probably because she wanted her children to get tough, knowing it was a hard world in the twenties and thirties.

The only light in the house was by candle or paraffin lamp, so it was always early to bed and early to rise. Then came electricity, grandfather had fought against it until he realised he could have a wireless, then the electric board could not put it in fast enough. He bothered them for days while they struggled to wire the house.

'Bloody wire', he used to moan, 'ugly bloody stuff, I don't want it hanging all over the place', but he settled down when the wires were set into the walls and under the floorboards. This was quite a revelation to him, the unseen power source, lurking all over his house, it took them both a long time to come to terms with it, but soon the smell of paraffin was gone and the house took on a different feel.

When the electricity was first installed in the house, Gran went around all the rooms with sticking plaster and put it over all the sockets for fear the electric would leak out, each night she would go up to the bedroom an hour before bedtime and turn on the light to air the room.

I found out in later life that grandfather used to beat her, she never complained once, I am sure she thought it was his right. In later years she had her revenge, it was always very subtle but it always made her smile.

CONSTIPATION

Poor Tom he couldn't go, you see he had a bit of trouble,
He used to sit in the little house and all he did was grumble.
But Jessie had the answer and to the chemist went,
She came back with the Syrup of Figs and put it by the bed.

Tom also had a nasty cough and cough mixture he took,
He kept it by the bedside next to his favourite book.
Jessie didn't notice, the bottles looked alike.
And when Tom started coughing it was very late at night.

When Jessie told the story, the tears they filled her eyes.
Her laughter was hysterical and she ached down both her sides.
When he woke up coughing and reached out for the bottle,
But in his rush to get relief, Syrup of Figs he swallowed.

The loo was up the garden then by the old pigsty,
And the sight of Tom running up the path put a gleam in Jessie's eye.

He rushed up to the little house to sit upon the seat,
As Jessie shouted after him 'put something on your feet'.

An hour went by and down the path he gingerly did tread,
Then in the house and up the stairs and carefully into bed.
Better now Jessie asked, as she smiled at his relief,
He did not utter word or sound he was afraid to sleep.

I never heard him cough again and Jessie didn't either,
She said she'd found a great cure to settle all his fever.
The cough mixture is still upstairs the bottle never opened,
He says that she should take it back and get her cash refunded.

Jessie sleeps well every night a grin upon her face,
Thinking of Tom going up the path at a racing pace.
The thought of it relaxes her and sends her off to sleep,
Dreaming of him running with nothing on his feet.

I used to watch her slicing bread, fearing she would cut her hand, she would hold the bread in her hand close to her chest, butter it and slice it towards herself, catch the slice by the corner and arrange it on a plate. The bread would be cut so thin and each slice would be perfect, I loved to see her slice bread.

When her children had grown up and moved on the household consisted of my grandmother, grandfather and David. David was born out of wedlock to daughter, Vera, this was a sin in grandfather's eyes but he and Gran raised David as their own. David and I were almost the same age but being brought up in totally different ways we never really got on, but we tolerated each other.

The taste of the home cured bacon and fresh eggs at my Ganddad's house was a real treat. He would keep a pig at the top of his garden, which was vast, the garden fed the family most of the year round and with Gran's chickens, for meat and eggs, and the occasional rabbits and fish, which came their way by means of his job, or a grateful shooter. Gran kept goats, which would only be milked by her, any attempt at an approach by anyone but her would be met with a head down charge. Father's brother Alan once shut my mother into the goat enclosure for a joke, mother did not take long getting out of the goats' territory, she never let Alan forget this and for years after she was still paying him back with some stunt or other.

With all they grew and reared they never went hungry, the pig was fed all the household scraps, not just from the Pheasantry but from the Manor house, perks of the job. This mixture was called swill, the pig was well looked after, it was never given a name except by the children but they were encouraged not to play by the pig sty for fear they would get too attached to it.

When the pig was big enough, Grandfather would go up the garden and light a big fire under a huge cast iron boiler and boil water. When the water was almost boiling, he would sharpen his knife and kill the pig, this was a particularly horrible affair. All the youngsters were banned from this ghastly sight and Grandfather was seen to shed a tear or two when the killing was due to take place, so he did have a soft spot but rarely showed it.

The pig would squeal and thresh about for a long time before it actually died. When it was dead and all the blood drained from its body, the hot water was poured over the pig to scald the hair off then it was shaved with a very sharp knife. This job called for all hands to help because the pig had grown to an enormous size. When the scalding was done, the pig was hoisted up onto a beam and gutted, the liver, lungs and heart were removed along with all intestines and stomach, all were used (I hope I'm not putting you off). The pig was then left to hang and dry out for a couple of days, during this time the offal, as the inners were called, would all be treated and processed, there would be faggots, chitlings, stuffed heart, some fry (liver) and the head, which was made into brawn. This was very tasty, and as long as you ignored what it was made from, you always ate your fill, the old people used to say, the only thing you can't eat from a pig is the squeal.

After a few days, the pig would be cut up and salted for bacon and ham. This was a long, skilful process and one I am proud to say, I learnt how to do, there would be a great feast of spare ribs and off cuts of pork. The joints of meat were covered in salt and left on a cold slab, turned now and again to make sure the salt penetrated the meat completely.

A few weeks later the meat would be removed from the salt and hung on the ceiling in the kitchen, this was where the family ate and sat in the evenings. The parlour or front room was always kept for very special occasions or laying out the dead.

Grandfather would tie flies for fishing, or make spinning minnows, or maybe a whistle. I still have a whistle he made, Grandmother would repair clothes, knit, or just sit and listen to the ticking of the clock, her eyes closed and a smile on her face. Grandfather often asked what she was smiling at but she never told him, maybe a secret lover from past times, I hope so.

TIC TOC

Tom was deafened by the guns,
So a hearing aid he had to have.
The first he had was not so good,
It ticked and tocked it drove him mad.

On the phone to his elder son,
Complaining this aid was done.
To his rescue he did come,
Really worried for his mum.

Jessie who was sitting there,
In her comfy rocking chair.
A smile across her gentle face,
Crocheting her lovely lace.

What's the matter with this thing?
Trying not to let a grin,
Jessie never showed a care.
While gently rocking in her chair.

It makes a noise all the while,
Tick and tock it drives me wild.
I've tried adjustments, by the book,
The bloody thing's just no good.

Jessie looks across and smiles,
He hasn't heard it for a while.
The tick and tock no fault at all,
He hears the clock on the wall.

For years the clock he has not heard,
And now it's getting on his nerves.
You've spoiled my fun now can't you see,
Never mind we'll have some tea.

The curing bacon was left for a few months more, all the time getting the flavour from the fire and Granddad's pipe smoke, *St Bruno Flake*. He would roll this tobacco in the palm of his hand, then when it reached the right consistency, carefully fill his pipe, packing it down just right, give a few sucks then with a spill from the fire he would light it, blow out long streams of grey smoke which would curl up to the bacon curing on the ceiling. When the bacon was finally ready, the taste was superb. And as if by magic another small pig would appear in the sty.

David, my cousin and I were playing by the river, which was just below the house. There was a man fishing and like most kids we were pestering him, he caught me and gave me a smack on the head and kicked my backside. David, who was a bit faster than I was escaped, anyway, as kids do, I thought it was my fault and told David not to say anything to Granddad for fear of getting more of the same punishment.

At teatime, which was religiously observed at four in the afternoon, and consisted of very thinly sliced bread and butter, with homemade jam and homemade cake with tea, David, who had a big mouth, told of the incident. Granddad got out of his chair and grabbed us both, demanding to know where this happened.

As we went through the door he picked up his gun, the gun was taller than me. We led him to the place where the man was still fishing. Granddad told both of us to hide behind the riverbank and wait for him, but, being kids we crept closer to see what he was going to do.

Granddad, gun under his arm, cartridges loaded in the barrels, with the gun in the broken position, strolled over to the fisherman and asked if he had a licence to fish, the man was very abusive and said he did not need a licence, again he was asked for his permit but started to get really angry. Without any warning Granddad brought the gun barrels up to the breech, raised his gun and shot the top of the man's fishing rod clean off, then he told the man to raise his arms and he marched him to the police station. I really thought he was going to kill him, this disturbed me so much and I never went to visit on my own again.

I never told my father or mother about this and my grandfather never mentioned it again. It was what was done, accepted, the way of things, to me it was like a scene from a cowboy film, sort of surreal but vividly real and very scary. I should have told my father of the incident, it was a very frightening experience. Neither David nor I ever spoke of it again but I am sure it had a lasting effect on David as it had on me. My Granddad died at the age of eighty and to his dying day he was a nasty old man, maybe it was the experiences he had in the first war that made him that way, I will never know. All I know is he gave my grandmother a very hard life.

FEAR

I thought he was going to shoot him,
That man with the fishing rod.
This little man with the great big gun,
With a face so stern and hard.
I dreamed of this for many years,
And woke up eyes full of tears,
He frightened me that little man,
For years and years and years.

David and I were never close, but at my father's funeral he was the only one of my father's family who came over and expressed his feelings and shook my hand; I thought a lot of that.

My Father

My father, Raymond, the oldest of the boys, was very much like his father, in looks as well as mannerism, hard and stern. He was raised up to be tough and he was, he served in the Royal Navy during the Second World War and saw action in most of the theatres of war, including Burma. He was once arrested for being drunk in charge of a telephone box in Durban, South Africa. I know very little of his war experiences and can only assume he had a hard time judging by his medals. He spent some time in Gibraltar at the Royal Naval Hospital and in a rehabilitation unit in Alexandria. The relationship I had with him was strained, we never saw eye to eye and I spent most of my time at home trying to avoid him.

He was a very clever man who could turn his hand to anything, he had learned the trade of interior builder and was, like his father, very clever. Most people saw him as a helpful and kind person who at the drop of a hat would rush to anybody's aid, day or night.

He was, for most of his working life, a maintenance engineer at the cottage hospital in Llandrindod and was very often called out in the middle of the night to repair something that had broken down or stopped working. He loved his job and had the respect of all who worked with him.

He was a bit of a ladies man and flirted with most of the hospital female staff he came into contact with. Each Christmas he would receive gifts of cake and puddings and the occasional bottle of scotch of which he was very fond but could not hold too much. I carried him to bed on many occasions but only at Christmas time. Mother used to get annoyed at his flirtatious behaviour and he would make it worse going on about all his ladies who relied on him.

One of my earliest memories of him was sitting at a homemade bench with a tin of tacks, some glue that smelt like petrol, a piece of thick leather, a curved knife, that I longed to get hold of but never did, and a cobbler's last. I still have the cobbler's last. The fire would be roaring, *The Archers* would be on the radio and father would set about repairing the family shoes. This he did with great skill, as his father had done and had probably taught him. He never taught me how to do this but I suppose he thought I was not that interested, on reflection I wish he had taken the time to talk to me, then he would have seen I was interested but too afraid to ask.

He had no time for guns and would not allow me a gun for years, until I finally wore him down with the aid of mother, but I was told if there was ever any complaints he would smash it into bits. He did love fishing and like his father he used to tie his own fishing flies and repair fishing rods as a hobby.

He never gave much of his time to me he was always too busy with other things that needed doing. He ignored me as much as possible giving all his attention to my sister, I did not mind this as I was closer to my mother. In some ways I am grateful for this because he gave me my independence early in life. I always seemed to be on the receiving end of any violence from him, the reason for this I never found out, he would lash out at the slightest excuse, I always seemed to be in the way. I think the abuse I suffered was a direct result of the war, I can find no other explanation for his violence.

My mother's parents were always on hand to lend an ear or help and my grandfather, Wally, (mother's father) who I used to call Poppa, was always there with a sympathetic ear and a penny for some sweets.

My beatings used to make Poppa very angry and he would have sorted things out if only for the sake of my mother's safety. He bit his tongue and offered refuge to me. The beatings got so bad at one time that I considered ending it all.

DARK THOUGHTS

At ten o'clock it's time for bed,
It's time to rest my weary head.
I lie in my bed, wide-awake,
Thinking of the mistakes I made.
At half past one, I'm still awake,
Wishing for dreams me to take,
But when I dream it's always bad,
Dreaming of the chances I had.
Too late for me I often say,
I wish the Lord would take me away.

~*~

Mother

My mother, Kathleen (Kitty) on the other hand was more forgiving when I was young, but she was very much under father's influence and did what was expected. She had a hard time sometimes calming father down after one of his 'turns' as his moods came to be known.

Mother was one of three girls, Lillian and Georgina were both younger, Georgina being only four years older than me, so she became my big sister, protecting me from any trouble I found myself in, often running to Nana to say I was having a bad time with father. She was my guardian angel on more than one occasion.

Mother could kick up a storm when she wanted and there were a few time when she lost it. When this happened father would remain very quiet, often retiring to the shed to mess around with his tools and let her settle down, she really frightened him, pity she didn't loose it more often, maybe I would not have had so many slaps. These arguments never involved violence between them but if I got in the way I got a slap just for good measure, never off mother though.

Mother's cooking was something to be marvelled at, especially her gravy, you had to stop the flow with a pair of scissors, a work of art could have been modelled out of this thick pale semi-liquid it was so thick. It would lie on your dinner like an eiderdown, never moving, daring you to try and eat it, but she could make a good Irish stew and her baking was wonderful.

She loved pottering about in the garden and needlepoint and was very fond of *Cadbury's Fruit and Nut* chocolate. On Sunday evenings when *Sunday Night at the London Palladium* was on the television she would treat herself to a half pound bar and devour it herself, guarding against father trying to steal a square or two.

When she was a young girl during the Second World War she had worked as an usherette in the Grand Pavilion. During the day she would clean house for a local minister, then in the afternoon help take out wounded soldiers for exercise and fresh air from the Ye Wells, this was a military hospital in Llandrindod. When I moved to Scotland in the late sixties I worked with a man who had spent some time in the Ye Wells during the war, furthermore he and mother had met.

Both my parents worked very hard at several jobs and consequently, I became a latch key kid, along with my sister. We would come home from school and fight, we never got on as kids, although we are now reasonably close.

In a lot of ways the term the 'good old days', was right, but in a lot of other ways it wasn't. Times were hard, even in the fifties and sixties, money was always tight and both parents, often had to work very long and hard in order to just survive. My father used to finish work and then go painting and decorating until late at night just to earn extra cash, and my mother used to wait on tables at local hotels to do the same. Even then it was hard to save and holidays were non-existent, unless we went to the seaside for the occasional day or two.

I remember it seemed to be the done thing, when I was young, to leap into a field full of cabbages or potatoes and just sort of lend a few, it wasn't considered real stealing. Scrumping apples or pears, strawberries and gooseberries, it was all fair game, of course it was stealing, but we were never greedy and you never did it for profit or sale.

Wally

My mother's father, Joseph Walter Gwyn Bunny, was one of the gentlest people I ever knew, he was always called Wally, or as we kids used to call him Popa. He came from the small market town of Rhayader in mid Wales. This little market town is at the foot of the Elan Valley where the vast reservoirs supply Birmingham with water. A village was flooded to create the Nantgwilt dam, when the dam is very low in water you can still see the faint outline of the village. Another dam, the Nantgro, was used by Barnes Wallis to test his bouncing bomb during the war in preparation for the great raids known as the dam busters, on the Mohne and Eder dams in Germany. The stone used to build the dams came from Glamorgan. Edward VII, and Queen Alexandra opened the first dams in 1904.

Wally's family moved to Builth Wells where they owned *The Lion Hotel.* He played football and rugby for Builth, but I know very little about his early life. He had one sister Victoria, she was feared by all the family, she had moved to Hereford when she was young, working with the Ministry of Defence, she then became private secretary to the owner of a munitions factory. She never married and after she retired her favourite pastime was annoying Nana, they had little time for each other.

When Popa, and Nana (the Greek) got married they moved to Llandrindod Wells where he became a chauffeur at a local garage the *Automobile Palace*. As the years went by he was promoted to forecourt manager.

His hobby was bowling, sport played a big part in his life he would follow all sorts with real enthusiasm. He used to spend hours at the Rock Park bowling greens, when he was allowed by Nana. He was also a very good snooker player; I still have a snooker cue presented to him by the great Joe Davies in 1928 for winning an amateur championship. He was a sergeant in the home guard during the Second World War; he was in the observer corps, but he never fought in the Great War, he was too young.

I can't remember a time when he raised his voice or lost his temper, his philosophy was to talk problems through. When we were young he used to occasionally hire a car and take the family off for a Sunday drive, usually to Amroth, where my grandmother's home was. The cars were very big, usually the very big Austin cars with little seats that folded out of the drivers and front passenger seat. Nana used to sit in the front seat and as we went through town, she would wave like the Queen at anybody she would see.

On one such excursion Nana was taken short and the car had to be stopped in order for her to relieve herself behind a hedgerow. Whilst she was crouched down a farmer, who was trimming the hedge and was unseen by her, commented how fine a day it was. Grandmother came leaping over the five bar gate yelling at Popa, 'Wally, start the car for goodness sake'. When she told of her experience Popa had to stop as he was laughing so much at her embarrassment he could not drive for laughing, needless to say it was a long time before she was allowed to forget this incident. If Nana had a bad mood on her as she often did (she was a hypochondriac), he would cheer her up reminding her of this, he would chuckle about it for years.

Popa used to collect silver paper and foil, this was sold and the money used to provide guide dogs for the blind, he was given some sort of award for this service but I can't remember what it was. Although his religion was Church of England one of his closest friends was a Roman Catholic priest, Father Barling, they could often be seen chatting and joking. When Popa died Father Barling took the service and arranged most of the funeral, I could not attend I was living in Scotland at the time.

Olive the Greek

Nana hated my father and he her, but they managed to hide it very well, possibly for the sake of keeping the peace. Nana maintained she was Greek, I have tried to find out if she was but with little success. She was born in the small village of Amroth in Pembrokeshire, overlooking the Bristol channel. The family home still stands on the cliffs, a reminder to the family of what we once owned and let go for a pittance but is now worth a small fortune. Amroth has, over the years, been taken by the sea, but a new sea wall has at last stopped the erosion. I still have distant relatives in the area, they have a cottage close to a village called Stepaside near to Wiseman's Bridge. This was the site of the rehearsal of the 1944 D day Invasion of Normandy, which was attended by Winston Churchill.

Nana, whose name was Olive, was a tall elegant woman with jet-black hair and smooth olive skin. Her family name was Nicholedies, this would bear out her claim to being Greek, or having Greek descendants. Her father Henry was at one time a prize bare knuckle fighter. He was according to Nana deported at the start of the Great War, only returning when hostilities had ceased. She never expanded on this story saying she could not remember much about it. He worked as a carter after the 1914/18 War and died in Amroth where he is buried.

Nana was, as were many of her generation prone to telling tales, usually getting times and dates mixed up, but I would sit and chat to her for hours, trying to piece together fragments of family tales in order to get some idea of where we came from unfortunately she gave little away about her side of the family, dark pasts maybe. The Pembrokeshire coast was renowned for smuggling, when I was young I often imagined her father with cutlass between his teeth, and rings in his ears.

She had three sisters Iris, Leticia and Nellie and one brother John (Jack). Nellie was drowned at a place locally known as Black Rock, off the Marros sands, she was collecting sea gulls eggs and was cut off by the tide. Her sister Iris lived and died in Pembroke dock, and Leticia married and moved to Spenymore in Co. Durham, where I still have distant relatives. Jack inherited the cliff house, being the oldest and only boy, he died in the house, followed shortly after by his wife, the house was sold and the money divided between his two children, Maurice and Shirly. Shirly lives in Stepaside cottage. All Nana left me was her recipe for corned beef pie, memories of cups of tea, cigarette smoke and tales of a bird called Mac mahout.

CRAZY MIXED UP GRANNY

Granny thought she was a Greek
And of this fact she'd often speak
About a bird called Mac Mahout
Who swore at vicars very rude.

About a prince who was kicked out
No arse in his trousers and not one pound
Who married a princess in a far off land
In order to lend a helping hand.

They had three sons and a daughter fair
I wonder if you have guessed where
But then old Granny was a Greek
And of such tales she'd often speak.

Nana always had the radio on, she loved music especially Kathleen Ferrier who sang a haunting song called *Blow the Wind Southerly*. This singer still haunts me, whenever I hear her singing I feel as though it is a voice from the grave, I blame Nana for these feelings. When I was a child, if Kathleen Ferrier was played on the radio she would cry, when I asked why, she would say 'because she is dead'. So if she was dead, how was she still singing? Try to explain this to a five year old who knows nothing of recordings, it really frightened me, I thought she was singing from her grave and her grave was inside Nana's radio.

Each day Nana would get ready and go to town, every day except Wednesday, which was half day closing, or Sunday when no shops opened. So at two o'clock on the dot we would set out to town, which was a reasonable walk. I only went with her on holidays or if I was off school with a cold or skiving. Anyway, we used to pass a place called the cottage where the garden was full of apple and pear trees. One apple tree had a branch that grew very close to the pavement. Every day Nana would look at a particular apple that was growing on the branch but just out of reach, she planned to pick that apple when it was ripe. Each day she gave it a longing glance and planned how she would obtain the fruit, which was forbidden to Adam, but she was determined to get. An umbrella, with a hooked handle was her means of obtaining said fruit, if she hooked the branch, she would be able to reach the apple.

So came the day, she checked no one was looking and with as much stealth as she could muster, she reached over with the umbrella and hooked it around the branch, gently starting to draw it near, just then a voice shouted, 'hey leave that apple alone!' She immediately withdrew and we set of up the road at almost a gallop. Not to be outdone she returned later that night armed with her ever-ready torch, and nicked the fruit by torchlight, what a woman. This was never mentioned to my grandfather but I'm sure he would have admired her stealth and cunning, she made the best corned beef pie I have ever tasted and her blackberry and apple pies were to die for.

STEALTH

Nana had to have that fruit
Of that she had decided.
So with the cunning of a fox
A plan she had contrived.

A brolly and a torch were used
And stealth to shame a cat.
With all the tools and a coat
She pulled low on her hat.

The night was still and silent
The torch it gave good light.
Nana nicked that apple
On that cold and chilly night.

I spent a lot of time with Nana, she always had a tale, a cup of tea and a welsh cake. Money was short in those days, the gas used for cooking was pre paid through a meter, which took shillings, a coin similar in size to a ten pence piece. Sometimes you ran out of shillings so other coins of a similar size found their way into the gas meter. If you got a piece of sandpaper and a halfpenny, which was slightly larger than a shilling, with a bit of patience you could sand it down to fit the meter.

Once a month the meter man, as he was called, came to empty it and you would have a small rebate as the tariff was always set high. As soon as the moneybox was opened the halfpennies would stand out against the silver of the shillings. The youngest child in the house always got the blame for putting them in the meter, but the meter man knew and said nothing, he gave the rebate, had a cup of tea and left, leaving the halfpennies, knowing he would find them again next month. This was known as fiddling the meter, but in no way was this ever abused.

HALFPENNIES

Don't you lose those halfpennies my Nana used to say,
I may run out of shillings to cook the tea one day.
And don't you tell the meter man what I keep them for,
So don't you lose those halfpennies
down the crack that's in the floor.

Such was Nana, she was a determined lady who got most of her own way, but worked hard at keeping a roof over the family's head.

Chapter Four

In 1965 I had left school, started my job as an apprentice butcher and fallen in love with the girl who was a nanny to the family who lived above the butcher's shop. Mary had long hair, short skirts and was a real tease, but I was scared to approach her, so I got nowhere. This happened a lot, I was always very shy, afraid of rejection, I only found out years later that Mary would have gone out with me if only I had asked her, by the time I found out she was married.

I had gained a few GCSE exams and fully intended to join the Royal Navy but I was still not sure I could take orders, so I put it on the back burner for a while, fully intending to join up at a later stage. Unfortunately the gas went out on the burner and I did not bother to re-light it. I would have liked to have been a professional golfer but was told by my father that I was being stupid, I suppose Jack Nicholas's father had told him the same, no matter. A job was the best option for the time being - what a mistake.

Life was just about to take a turn for the worst. I was apprenticed to a local family butchering business, what a joke, what a half arsed place it was, no-one was qualified. I was paid half a crown for each hour worked and I *was* worked. I did everything from sweeping the floor to getting the tea.

The manager at the shop was a man called Jack Mostyn, he was a good boss to me but skilled in what later came to be known as knacker butchering. He was a man of very restrictive size due probably to the amount of cigarettes he smoked, we used to joke about him having duck's disease, his backside was too close to the ground.

The boss I was eventually going to work for was still enjoying his freedom, he hated Jack and made no bones (pun) about the fact, as soon as he was in total charge he was going to sack him. Jack hated him as well, calling him a jumped up squirt and shouting abuse at him whenever he got the chance, this made working there amusing in a lot of ways as the rows went on for days.

Bob Knill, the jumped up squirt, was still being a bit of a playboy, as much as anybody could be a playboy in a backwater sort of town, and courting all the girls he could before the reins were tightened on him and bought him to heel.

The Knill family on the whole were very nice people although they owned a fair amount of land, property and other businesses, they were down to earth country people. Then there was Bob. For the most part he was a kind and helpful sort of person but he had a wild streak, he would fly off the handle at the slightest thing, usually anything to do with Jack Mostyn.

I was very fond of Bob, for a long time he was a sort of surrogate brother and helped me in a lot of ways when I was starting out in the meat industry, but he changed when his father died, he lost the ability to be a human being. It was as if a Jekell and Hyde mood would take over he, would fly into a rage at the slightest thing and if the problem got out of hand he would lose control of his speech, he would stutter uncontrollably almost taking on the appearance of having a fit without the convulsions.

True as his word after his father's funeral, his father being in control of all the businesses, the butchers shop being only a small part of the empire, he came into the shop and sacked Jack and left me in charge until he got himself organised. He became arrogant and a bully and took great delight in throwing his weight about, a great pity he changed in that way, but I stuck it out, all the time hoping he would eventually come to his senses and realise that everyone who worked for him were trying to help.

I was sent to Hereford every Monday to technical collage, this bus ride on the old Black and White coaches took two hours, it was only forty miles away but it seemed like four hundred, the college was in Newtown Road, Hereford. I had been to Hereford several times before I attended the collage so it was not a strange town to me, so off I went with my case full of knives and notebook, only to find the collage was a collection of old Nissan huts left over from the war. I was to learn the trade of butchering here, then on Tuesday, teach my boss what I had learned the day before.

My tutor in college was John Carver, he came from Bartestry Cross just outside Hereford I thought he had a good name for a butcher, he had not a hair on his head, we nicknamed him Curly. He taught all of us in his charge all he knew from how to cut and price to receipts for all sorts of by products. Some Mondays he could not get to college so we went to a coffee bar called the Cabin or went to the pictures, but Curly would make sure we worked doubly hard the next week in order to make up for lost time.

The day started at eight in the morning the first job being to cut meat and dress the window, then there were sausages to make, orders to be made up and delivered, serving in the shop and keeping Jack's cigarette ends out of sight.

For the greater part I liked my job, I met lots of people and got a reasonable reputation for my work. I particularly enjoyed the window dressing, especially at Easter and Christmas, then at the end of each day the window would be emptied and scrubbed, the wooden block would be scraped with a wire brush the floor mopped and home for six-thirty. The shop work was only a part of my job, slaughtering was the other part. The slaughterhouse was at the rear of the shop in Tudor Lane. Monday was the day for killing the animals, which were to supply the meat to the butcher's shop, 'slaughtering day' it was not the nicest of jobs.

I recall the first thing I killed, my hands were shaking so much I could barely hold the knife, the sudden rush of blood from the animal was hot and steaming, running across the floor was the life of this poor animal I had killed, I felt sick. I was told you get used to it, I don't think I ever did.

The method of killing was, in hindsight, cruel, we were supposed to stun the animals before slitting their throats and letting the blood. The stunning could take one of two methods, you could shoot the animal with a captive bolt gun .22 calibre, this method had to be used for cattle but sheep were laid on what was called a cratch, your knee pressed hard against their terrified body holding them down, then it was a swift cut, the knife going in just behind the ear and coming out just behind the other ear, then you would swiftly break the animals neck feeling the bones part with a crack. Pigs were mostly electrocuted by means of stunning tongs which would be clamped around its head, a button on the tongs pressed and the pig was electrocuted, then its throat was slit, the pig threshed about for several minutes before finally shaking itself into death stiffening for the last throws of its life as if it were trying to summon up strength to get up and run. Just before killing the pigs they would squeal and scream knowing what was to come. One of my regrets in life is killing so many animals, I should never have continued in this career but I found myself somehow trapped. Since leaving it, I could never go back, I would find it too upsetting.

My boss's grandfather who worked with us taught me when he was able. He was shell shocked in the Great War. Whenever there was a thunderstorm, he would just fall asleep, I think it was a reaction to the noise that set him off, he was a kind man of eighty years and had in his life seen some terrible things. He would tell jokes and keep us laughing all day, the stories would seem never ending and for a man of his age he was surprisingly strong, he was a game old man and taught me well. His name was Harry Tomlinson, he and Doug Price, who nicknamed me Dango, why I don't know, set about teaching me how to skin and dress carcasses, starting at the bottom cleaning the intestines and dealing with the offal, washing floors and stacking skins and pelts.

Bob put in some time at the killing but he would disappear for long periods of time, he would rush for about ten minuets then disappear again leaving the three of us to finish the work and clean up, sometimes this was nine o'clock at night, we all started at eight in the morning. He would wander in around lunchtime and make a big show rushing around then disappear for an hour to talk on the phone leaving Doug and me to finish the work, we did not mind as he somehow upset the balance of work we would manage better without him.

Then came motorbikes. It started with an old 125cc Royal Enfield motorcycle with a hand change gearbox. This bike belonged to Peter Edwards who later changed his name to Elvis Presley (more of him later). The feeling of being propelled at breakneck speed of 25mph with the wind in my face and not having to peddle like a dervish was exhilarating. I thought, "if I can maintain this for the rest of my life I will be on a winner."

Well that dream came a cropper. I have always had the knack of finding trouble, on that day it was a hedge, the introduction was me being unceremoniously driven through it not being able to let go of the bike. I dragged myself and the bike out of the hedge, I vowed two things that day, first get a crash helmet and second to look where I was going. I have never lost my love of motorbikes although over the years I came many croppers, mostly off motorbikes, I have always hankered after a Harley Davidson but we all have our pipe dreams.

CROPPER

I often came a cropper off the motorbike.
It's not something you get used too or get to like
But on you go, no matter what, and ride it like a twerp
And then you fall off again and feel a bloody jerk.

About this time I got my first legal road motorbike. It was a 1952 yellow BSA Bantam 175 cc, hand painted, bought from a local dealer, John Davies, what a heap, 30 mph, with a strong wind behind you. I had it for about six weeks then changed it for a 250 cc, Royal Enfield, a much better bike.

I used to deliver the daily meat orders on my motorbike, I never got paid petrol for this but Jack Mostyn would see me all right. I used to call into Nana's for a cup of tea and a biscuit, and a job that should have taken half an hour usually took an hour, Jack turned a blind eye to this.

I was learning to drive around the same time, we had an Austin A35 van at work which was used by Bob for his romantic assignations. How the hell any girl would get into that stinking meat van amazed me but he was out on the razz every night causing his late starts for work. He would turn up each morning, go to the toilet and throw up, he would then go home for breakfast and possibly come back around lunchtime, use the phone and disappear for the rest of the day, usually to a local livestock market or to a farm to see some stock.

I started to drive this A35 van in and out of the yard to wash it and clean it out, I used to hit the gate post regularly. I would get a bollocking, each time I hit the post, but after a while I got it into the yard without hitting anything.

Bob was very helpful at this time he started to teach me to drive legally, he would get into the shop van tell me where I was going then fall asleep, probably out of fear, he was bad tempered, persistent and arrogant but he got me through my test first time and for that I thank him.

Father had a Morris traveller, a lovely car, Wedgwood blue with wooden body trim, it had red mock leather seats and chrome headlight covers. It had a roof rack painted the same colour as the car, he had bought new carpets for it and a thing that fitted onto the driver's door so he could drive with the window open and not get any draught. It also had chrome wheel discs and the tyres were painted with black tyre paint, it was his pride and joy, he spent hours washing and polishing it. He would let cousin David drive it but never me, he never thought I was capable. When I challenged him about this, he beat me up so badly I could hardly walk, saying David was far cleverer than I was so he could drive his car.

The one time he let me drive it, I crashed it, no matter how I protested to him it was not done on purpose, he never believed me. I ran into the back of a car that had stopped for pigeons feeding in the road. I borrowed it to go and get mother some cigarettes from the local shop and on the way I picked up Peter Edwards. I was showing off not taking enough notice of what was going on around me and probably speeding.

Father was not happy, he was too angry to try and get hold of me, he was hysterical, he threatened me with all sorts of physical violence. I had to promise to sell my motorbike to help pay for the car. Swift justice was forthcoming, again this was not planned, I had to take my licence to the police station after the accident, on my return I was knocked off my Enfield and ended up in hospital, end of Enfield, life certainly was taking me for a dangerous ride that week.

Father was not happy, in fact he went crazy. I was lying in hospital with a badly mangled ankle and foot, he stood at the bottom of the bed and tore into me verbally with such a tirade of abuse he had to be escorted out of the hospital by the matron, thank God for Matron Green. I thought my time on earth was getting very close to the end. On her return she looked at me over the top of her half rimmed glasses and said "I think you have upset your father", she was not wrong, I paid for my crash in more ways than one. He never forgave me I was never allowed to drive his car again. The insurance repaired the car as good as new but when he got it back he refused to drive it so it was changed.

I came out of hospital to be faced daily with a tirade of abuse as to how useless I was, I was beginning to believe this myself, in his eyes I could do nothing right. I began to doubt my parentage at this point and asked Nana if I was his son or had mother had an affair before they married? She never answered my question but said she would talk to Popa about it, Popa had a very stern talk with father and the daily humiliation stopped. I was going to go the first chance I got, sod him and his temper, David could have all his attention I did not need him, I never did after that, I would get on with it myself.

SMILE

When somebody does you wrong
and gets right up your nose,
Just shrug it off, get on with life,
and keep right on your toes.
Don't dwell on things that are long past,
leave them well behind,
For if you don't, they surely will,
slowly taint you mind.

So when somebody does you wrong,
don't forget to smile,
It does your heart a power of good
and makes them really wild.
Think of their anger, have a smile
and have a giggle,
The minds of those that lose their head
are something of a squiggle.

And at the end of every night,
when to your bed you go,
Think of those that pissed you off
and let your mind just go.
They're the ones with all the grief,
they're really in a tangle,
You're safely tucked up in your bed
and they are in a mangle.

Friends

There seemed to be a lot of Peters around, I had three close friends all called Peter, so nicknames had to be adopted. Peter Brooks was a special friend, he was deaf, so he remained Peter, this made life easier for him. He was a carpenter and a very good one, his father was the general manager of the biggest garage in town the Automobile Palace, he was very kind to all of us who befriended Peter but I was closer to Peter than anyone and we became inseparable. He'd just got his first motorbike, a Triumph Tiger Cub, it was a really nice bike, although it was comparatively small in size its power was big, we were all green with envy. I taught Peter to talk a little, we spent many hours together, either at the cinema or riding our bikes exploring various towns. The fact he could not hear anything I said did not affect us, he could lip read as fast as I could talk. I was the one who had difficulty, although to see us together you would never be able to tell that Peter was deaf, he taught me to sign a little but it is a skill I unfortunately no longer have, I should learn it again. He had been educated at the local residential school for the deaf, there were several hundred deaf children at the school, but sadly it closed due to lack of funding. This was quite a blow to the town as the school brought in a lot of revenue, also Peter was losing a lot of friends, this upset him for a time but he soon became one of the boys and we had many great times together.

Peter number two was Peter Evans, we nicknamed him Bally, I can't remember why. He was a flash git, always smart, best of clothes paid for by a doting mother who thought the sun shone out of his arse. He was not into motorbikes, they were too dirty for him and, as his mother often preached, you don't want to get involved with those rough types. Bally never amounted to much except at the local golf club. I don't think it was his game, more to do with the amount of cash he flashed around. He thought he was too good for us but he always hung around so we tolerated him. When we went to the pub he would drink shorts, whereas we all drank beer, his saving grace was that he could pull the girls so we kept him close. He had a habit of turning up at the most inopportune times, just as you had pulled a girl, he would appear and bugger it all up, but that was Bally, he was the best looking and always had the most cash, thanks to his doting mother he would flash the cash and the birds would fly to him. He was a lazy sod, his mother spoilt him rotten and his father chucked him out, suitcase on the doorstep job. He lived with us for a while until he crawled back home begging forgiveness but was only allowed back home if he got a job, so he went to work in a garden centre. He was at home with the plants.

FLASH GIT

He was as smart as any model,
always talking lots of twaddle.
Best of clothes he did wear,
didn't have a single care.

Until his dad chucked him out,
get a job you lazy lout!
He lived with us a little while,
but with no money lost his style.

Back to Dad apologies,
almost on his bended knees.
Working now with lots of plants,
got to pay for flashy pants.

The other Peter, Peter Edwards had his name changed to Eddy, he was a real mad ass, he would do almost anything for a bet. He was only five foot tall in his socks, we were all heading for six foot, but like all small people, he had something to prove. He would pick a fight with anybody, the bigger the better, he always got hammered but he kept on coming, he did not know when to stop and we had to drag him away before he got really hurt on more than one occasion. He always had a cigarette in his mouth and a razor in his pocket, he would light one cigarette from the other, a real chain smoker, we all wondered where he got all his money from but we never found out. We all smoked then and very often when you did not have a smoke you would share one, except with Eddy, he always made a duck's arse of his, that is he used to get the end very wet, so he never got asked to share. He had a way with girls but mostly very young impressionable ones, we called them jail bait. In later life he changed his name to Elvis Presley and dyed his hair from almost white blond to matt black, he believed he was a reincarnation of Elvis, what a nutter. I don't know why we all bothered with him really he was always causing trouble but we had all grown up together and we were mates come good or bad.

When Elvis died, personally it was a small incident in my life, but others got really upset and still mourn the passing of the one they called the King. I think it is a matter of opinion but each to his own, anyway the Elvis I knew saved his money and went to Gracelands to see the resting place of the legendary singer. He saw Elvis's grave, did the tour of Memphis, saw Sun recording studios, he was well pleased and sorry to leave his hero's last resting place. On his return journey he was delayed at Kennedy airport, a Russian ballerina was claiming political asylum so his flight was delayed.

Before he went to America, he had asked me, to pick his wife up and meet him at the airport, I agreed. I had been married and divorced by this time, my wife Anne had left me, and I was courting again, her name was Wendy. We had no idea which flight he was on, all we had was an approximate time, we were three country hicks surrounded by thousands of people, moving staircases, moving walkways, loudspeaker tannoys, this was a city. We found the terminal and were told there had been a delay in New York owing to this Russian ballerina and our passenger might have got on a different flight to the one we were supposed to meet. We were in a totally alien environment, looking for a guy called Elvis, who was five feet tall with blackboard coloured hair, light blond eyebrows and sideburns stuck on with theatre make up glue, in an Elvis jump suit that was a size too big. We waited and waited, no sign of the elusive Elvis, plane after plane arrived, again and again, we rushed to the arrivals gate, no Elvis. Lunch came and went, with each of us taking it in turns to eat and use the toilet, I went up to the enquires desk and waited, in a never-ending queue, wondering what I was going to say to the very attractive lady who was giving out messages on the tannoy.

"Um yes," I stuttered, "can you help me please, I know this is going to sound very strange to you, but I am supposed to be meeting a passenger arriving from New York, I'm afraid, we may have missed him so could you please put out a call for him?" "Certainly sir, what's the passenger's name?"

"Elvis Presley."

She almost laughed in my face, I beat her to it. "Honestly, that is his name, he changed it by deed poll and he refuses to answer to anything else."

She looked at her colleague then, lifting the microphone up, she said in a clear voice, "Would Elvis Presley please report to the enquiry desk and make yourself known."

The hush that suddenly descended on the whole room was deafening. All eyes seemed to be on me, to say I was embarrassed would be an understatement. Then out of the blue Elvis appeared, I introduced him to the lady who had put out the call for him, she looked at him and burst into uncontrollable laughter as did her companion. I think they were expecting a hunk instead of this short arsed little squirt. We quickly made our exit from Heathrow, all the time Elvis was asking what they were laughing at and none of us ever told him, I think it was out of pity, he did look a sight.

ELVIS

Elvis is alive, you see him everywhere,
he's down the local chip shop or working at the fair.
Everybody knows him, he swaggers and he swanks,
I think he would be better off, back home with the Yanks.

How many folk do you know who think they are Elvis?
Dressing in that jump suit and swinging at the pelvis.
Hairstyle that never moves and sideburns stuck so tight,
Come and hear him singing, he's down the pub tonight.

I never did like Elvis, I couldn't take his tunes,
they never really moved me, except out of the room.
I never bought his records or saw any of his films,
I used to ride my motorbike and get a lot more thrills.

So if you do see Elvis, give him all my best,
Tell him that he's fabulous and that he was the best.
But tell him that he should be in that place up in the sky,
Singing to the angels, not waiting for chips to fry.

Clive Howells was the very first friend I made in Oxford Road Primary School.

He ended it all when he was 20 years old, I think of Clive even now, I have a picture in my mind of him on his motorcycle with a home rolled *Golden Virginia* cigarette in his mouth and not a care in the world. We all respected Clive, he was a clever mechanic, if there was a problem with any of our bikes Clive could fix it, he never let on he had problems, he must have had to have ended it all although he never spoke of them, I wish he had then maybe he would be here today. What a waste. He hung himself from a railway bridge close to a place we all knew as Howey Docks. Howey is a village outside Llandrindod on the road to Builth Wells. Clive was being bullied at work, he was a big chap, quite capable of looking after himself but he was never confrontational and always walked away from arguments. I never once saw him loose his temper with another person although he used to loose it when he fell off his bike. He only wanted a quiet life, one of the men he worked with was always picking on him, I suppose it got so bad he decided life was not worth living. The bully was a grown man his name was Guthrie James.

Clive's father was a sales rep for *Lions Cakes*, why this has just come into my mind is because I have just eaten a piece of cake with a cup of tea and the taste of those out of date *Lions Cakes* that Clive used to bring and distribute was once again in my mouth. The cakes were not exactly stale, just a little dry and had a flavour all of their own, its strange how smells and tastes take you back to your childhood. Clive is buried in a little churchyard in Disserth, a village between Howey and Newbridge-On-Wye, he rests under a Yew tree in the shade. I could not get to his funeral as I was living in Scotland at the time, but a wreath made into the shape of a motorbike was arranged and everyone who knew him, except me, attended. It was many years before I plucked up the courage to visit his grave and I shed a few tears that day.

Jeremy was another great friend, we grew up together and remained solid friends all our lives. Like most of us, Jem was mad about motorbikes, he owned a Dot trials bike. This was the bike to have, a real trials bike of the greatest calibre and we were all very envious of him and his Dot. None of us ever got to ride it, he kept it polished and hardly ever took it into the mud, he was so proud of it. He was trained as a *Rolls Royce* engineer, his skill with machinery was superb. Jeremy's father established a hardware store in the town, and his sister ran the shop for years but when she finely got married, Jem took over the shop.

Jem's downfall was committees, he was on everything from motorcycle trials to the council and Round Table. He devoted himself to the well-being of the town and was involved in everything he could be. I was proud, to be best man at his wedding, it was a grand occasion. Top hat and tails, horses and carriages, it was a day to remember. Nicky, his bride, looked a picture and the day went well.

When we moved to South Wales, we lost touch for a few years, then one day the phone rang, the caller said Jem had fallen off a ladder. He had been taking the town's Christmas decorations down and was up a ladder, holding a string of lights that stretched across the main street, when the weight of them pulled him backwards off the ladder, he fell about thirty feet onto the road. He did not survive the fall suffering serious head injuries. I was a bearer at his funeral and it seemed to me that a part of me was being buried with Jem, one my generation. I was beginning to realise how vulnerable I was. I cried for Jem inwardly, tears were not fitting, but it opened my eyes and I think it was then I decided to live for the day. The whole town turned out for Jem's funeral, I never realised how much he was loved and respected by the town, I felt very humble and sad. He left a wife and two daughters who, may I say, are doing him proud and he will certainly live on through them, they are a credit to his memory.

TAKE CARE

It always seems to happen, when good turns you do,
If something's going to happen, it is usually to you.
So when you volunteer, some tasks to undertake,
Always think of safety and great care you take.

Rewards are not in heaven, no matter what we're told,
The best reward in this life, is getting to grow old.
To watch your children grow, and get a good career,
Than have to struggle, on their own with no one there to steer.

~*~

Just a touch on the sixties

In 1966 my first four wheel transport cost £29.00, a Ford 100e van. I was cooking, this was luxury, it had a heater and plenty of room in the back, which was partitioned off with a sheet of plywood for privacy, know what I mean, nudge, nudge! The flash git was hanging on then, he had no wheels so I was a taxi, I didn't mind, I had a new found freedom, as long as he paid his share of the petrol. Many nights were spent in Smoky Joes Café, this used to be Bouncing Bob's shop, which had long since closed and converted into a dive of a café

With the van and a liberal coating of *Brylcream* we would hang around the café in the hope of picking up a couple of girls. The van was called the tart trap, it only had three gears, the windscreen wipers worked on a compressed air system which worked well when you drove slowly but if you speeded up in a rain storm they would go very slowly and sometimes stop altogether. I had a pair of ram's horns wired to the front grill and a Welsh flag stuck across the back doors, a radio which sometimes worked tuned into Radio Luxemburg and hairy seat covers. The back was carpeted and an 'L' plate was stuck for some reason on the roof inside, it was my refuge from the torment of the day.

Have you ever reflected on the past, when you think of all the friends you suddenly acquired when you have something no one else had? The van was well used and very soon it was attracting the attention of the local constabulary, which seemed to take great delight in stopping us to check documents and how many were riding in the back. On one occasion I took my documents into the police station and asked them to keep them there as they seemed to want to see them more than I did, I was not stopped so much after that.

People say you had to have lived in the sixties to appreciate them, this is true, if you missed the sixties you missed, in my opinion, one of the most exciting times of all. I was at my juvenile best in the sixties. Rock and roll was giving way to pop music, Bill Halley and the Comets were fading and the Beatles were on the march, flower power and the hippy movement were growing and Scott McKenzie sang about San Francisco. The BeeGees, singing falsetto as if their underpants were too tight, the Walker Brothers, Englebert Humperdink, Tom Jones were all just starting to make a mark. Discos were all the rage with psychedelic lighting. *Top of the Pops* burst onto our television screens with Pans People and Jimmy Savile. Programs such as the *Billy Cotton Band Show* were still on television and Russ Conway tinkled the ivories. Radio Luxemburg was getting less popular as was Radio Caroline, and Radio One was launched with Tony Blackburn as the first D.J. What a difference that made, the light program had gripped us for too long, the strained tones of Frankie Vaughn and Alma Cogan were excruciating. Although there were those like Dickey Valentine and Matt Monroe, of whom Frank Sinatra said 'he is the only Limey who can sing' were at least kept on Radio One.

There were Mods (motor scooters) and Rockers (motorcycles), coffee bars, frothy coffee a great invention served in most Brachie café's, steamed pies, chips and Coca Cola, (this drink swallowed with a couple of Aspirin had a strange effect on people). 'Make Love Not War' was the slogan of the day and believe me we all tried.

Things were great. Or were they?

Drugs were making more of an appearance, L.S.D was out of the shadows where it had been for a long time, it was trendy, it was cool, it was bloody stupid! Thank goodness I never had the need to try it. Under age drinking was rife, pubs had back rooms away from the main bar for the under age drinkers, landlords made a lot of money out of us then. Gangs were starting to get territorial and serious clashes would frequently break out, the clashes between Mods and Rockers were becoming very serious, the courts were full of thugs. And condoms were never used, the sheer embarrassment of asking for them was enough, "something for the weekend sir?"

Pop groups and rock bands grew at an amazing rate, the Top Ten was a fiddle, groups like The Who used to smash their instruments on the stage and actors ran around in the nude in a production called *Hair*. What a time. Jimmy Hendrix was acclaimed the greatest rock guitarist of all time, but died of a heart attack induced by an overdose of drugs, choking on his own vomit. The Rolling Stones were publicly admitting to using drugs, one of them even jumped out of a widow and killed himself. Most of the top groups were taking drugs or had some involvement in them. Motown was the new American sound all the way from Detroit, The Supremes, The Beach Boys, The Mammas and Papas were the best thing to come out of America.

You could, immigrate to Australia, for ten quid. Liverpool was the capital of the world Jerry Marsden wrote the national anthem of Liverpool, "You'll Never Walk Alone", and Dusty Springfield sang soul as it had never been sung before.

There was the Cuban crisis, the assassination of President John F Kennedy; I bet you can remember where you were on that day? Man walked on the moon, America went to war with Vietnam. And the man with the greatest dream of all time was assassinated in Memphis; Dr Martin Luther King, I wonder what heights he may have reached had he lived.

Elvis, fought back on the record front and Cliff Richard did a wonderful impression of him. Vincent Price and Peter Cushing were the horror movie heroes and the Lone Ranger and Tonto ruled the Wild West. Harold Wilson was the prime minister who believed he ruled the U.K. The Russian spy ring was exposed with Anthony Blunt and Bertram Russell. There was 'Ban the Bomb', Christine Keeler and John Profumo in sex for secrets. Lady Chatterley's Lover hit the bookshops at last as a legal publication no more to be sold under the counter. Parade magazine was published with the first pictures of topless girls, possibly the forerunner of Playboy magazine.

The world had suddenly started to wake up in the field of technology, cars started to get sleeker and faster, jet aircraft travel was the in thing if you had the money, and foreign holidays were becoming more affordable. People were beginning to buy their own homes and Mary Quant launched the mini skirt. Elizabeth David changed our view on food with more adventurous food writing, and a day at the seaside was still a treat. And I passed my motorcycle and car test, life was reasonably good

All in all I think the sixties were an age apart, far removed from reality in a lot of ways, but what an impression they left those of us who experienced them.

TIME

Always, make an effort,
no matter how hard it is.
For if you stand and waste your time,
your life goes like a fizzzzzzzzzz.

You may fall on your tail sometimes,
and pride it takes a fall.

So get up off the ground you nit,
Get your back against the wall.
Remember all the friends you make,
on your lofty climb.
You may need them on the way down,
on your rise just take your time.

Smell the roses on the way,
and lend a helping hand.
Tell your friends your problems,
they all will understand.

Time it goes so slowly
when you're young at play.
But when you're old and slower,
Your life seems just a day.

Chapter Five
SCOTLAND

1968 and things at home were taking a turn for the worse, relationships with my father were so strained that every time I saw him coming home, I would head in the other direction.

We were at loggerheads, I could do nothing right. He came home one afternoon just as I was going out on my motorbike, my hair was long and it stuck out from underneath my helmet, he physically dragged me to the barbers and sat there and waited while I had my hair cut, humiliating or what? That was the last time he ever laid a hand on me from then on I fought back. I'd had enough of being treated like an idiot, I may have been a little thick at times I hold my hand up to this but I was not going to take anymore shit off anyone, least of all off someone who was supposed to love me as I was his son.

I rebelled I lost interest in myself, my self-esteem was on the floor and I was beginning to plan a move away from all this nonsense. Then I met Anne, she was on the road having run away from home and was sort of travelling around the country. We fell in love, well maybe it wasn't love but a way out of my situation, so I moved to Scotland, I did not tell anyone I was going I just packed a bag and went.

Anne was from a village called Findhorn on the Moray Firth, six hundred inhabitants, and five hundred miles away. She made up with her family and I was thanked for bringing her home, little did they know that I was on the run so to speak, but I was free of my father, for the first time in my life I felt freedom and I liked what I was feeling.

Scotland was a foreign place, would I need my passport? Would

I get a stamp on my passport? No stamp, Scotland was different, I did not realise how different, the food, the people, accents, traditions, licensing hours, the pubs closed at ten and carry outs would be purchased and you went to a party. Life was so different, people were on the whole very friendly except one or two who did not take to interlopers, but I soon made friends with all. I was Taffy, I had never been called taffy in my life before, I was eighteen years old, life was suddenly going to get a whole lot harder. To top it all Anne's mother took an instant dislike to me, Anne always said she had run away because her mother was jealous of her relationship with her father, they were very close she was the apple of his eye, being the only child, her mother refused to have more than one, so when I arrived on the scene with Anne I was deemed the ogre who had returned with the prodigal daughter, who she never thought to see again, I had spoiled her dream of a life without ties.

Out of the frying pan.

When Anne and I ran away, I was unaware of her illness, she hid it well. She was an alcoholic and I'm afraid I did not cope with it very well when I did find out. We did our best to work the problem through, but it was very hard, both on Anne and myself. It came to the point where I did not want to go home for fear of what I might find, the first clue I had was I had started to collect miniature bottles of whiskey and had a reasonable collection in a display cabinet I had built, I was showing my collection to a friend when I noticed one or two of the bottles had the seal broken, when I inspected them I found they contained cold tea instead of whiskey. I asked Anne if she knew how this had happened and she denied all knowledge of it, this was the first time I suspected things were not right. After this I must admit I forgot about it for a long time, although when we went out I noticed she could drink more than any man in the pub and still remain reasonably sober, her father commented on this on more than one occasion but we did not dream she was an alcoholic, this realisation came much later.

We had a daughter, Vicky; she was born in March 1969, in a hospital in Forres. She was so pretty and small, I wondered what we were bringing her in to.

It was very hard to cope, a new baby, an alcoholic wife and a mother-in-law who would have taken out a contract on me if she knew how to go about it. I was cycling to work each day seven miles each way rain or shine, money was tight and it seemed the more I earned the more Anne spent.

I was too immature to ask for help, her father Hugh had no idea of Anne's illness, although I had a sneaky suspicion her mother did, I could not bring myself to talk to him about it, I thought I could cope with all the problems, as I suppose most young people do, but if I had not been so proud and asked, maybe things would have been different. But I was, so to speak, in a foreign land, where the whiskey was the elixir of life, and as such, no one seemed to bother too much about the occasional drunk, unless they fell down in the street in front of them in which case they would have to step over them risking a fall.

I had no close friends that I could confide in at that time, so everything was kept secret. She had an Auntie Whinne, her father's sister, she could sink a drop or two, who was married to Bob he was a hopeless alcoholic, but he was always cheerful and never missed a day's work through his illness he seemed to have it under control, so I hoped Anne would follow this path, alas, she did not. I voiced my concerns to her Auntie Margaret, her father's other sister, who was not the most approachable of people but I knew I would get a positive response from her, she said to ignore it as it was probably post natal depression and she would soon get over it, she did not.

The first job I had in Scotland, which led to my partial acceptance in the village was working on the fishing. I had never seen fishing on such a scale, trawling for salmon, I worked with a team from Peterhead, a town just north of Aberdeen I could not understand a word they said for the first six weeks but I liked the job and soon got on with all I worked with save one. He was a real ladies man, one of two brothers, Ewan and Arnold Anderson from Aberdeen. Arnold was best man when Anne and I got married, he was the foreman on the fishing gang and took me under his wing and taught me what I needed to know about fishing. Ewan, who was older, was bitterly jealous of this fact, they would fight all the time, physically and verbally, sometimes throwing each other into the sea. I stepped over the mark one day and told them they were acting like kids, Arnold laughed but Ewan took real offence at my interruption into the continual row over the Foreman's job, but when I introduced him to Anne's cousin Mary he forgave me and fell in love with her, but only for the fishing season.

I have a great admiration for all those who make there living from the sea. These were hard men well used to the salt on their hands and the wind and rain. I was not and for the first week or so my hands were raw, they were very painful but I soon got used to salt, wind and rain. The season was from February to September and it was all over all to soon, I really liked the fishing.

SALTY

Fishing for a living was a smashing way of life,
to be away from all the strains of this modern life.
Sailing on the sea so wide and tasting salt all day,
Pulling nets so full of fish whilst sailing far away.

Spare a thought for fishermen they work so very hard,
Battling the stormy seas repairing nets and spars.
Just to catch the fish you like with your bag of chips,
So bear a thought for fishermen and their little ships.

I then started work with Wimpy Buildings in Forres, I was a scaffolder's mate and dumper truck driver. This was when Ian Paisley raised his head, as most of the workers were Irish they left the building sites and returned to Ireland, leaving a skeleton crew to finish the work, which was sadly behind schedule. So the site closed and I was transferred to RAF Kinloss, only five miles from home to start work steel erecting. The building we worked on was a simulator for the new Nimrod aircraft, which was to replace the much-outdated Shackelton. I was making progress, from scaffolder's mate to steel erector, a step up so to speak.

When that job finished I worked for a heating engineering company from Aberdeen, Hayden Young, still at RAF Kinloss. I had a car by this time, an old Morris Minor I had bought whilst in Wales visiting, we had taken Vicky down to show her off. The problem with father had abated slightly and he was using mother as sort of blackmail, saying she was desperate to see her new granddaughter. We went down on the train, while we were back in Wales a friend had a car which was too cheap to refuse, so we bought it and drove it back to Scotland, no tax or insurance but we got home safely.

The new job with Hayden Young was great, I was learning new skills, they taught me to weld and I did a fair bit of steel erecting. I was scaffolding for a while and helping to install heater panels in the roof of the hangers. It was hard work, I hankered after the fishing, as the season had started again but the money was not enough. I enjoyed my jobs as much for the experience as the company. Working with all these different people I gained a wealth of experience, in all matters - building and life.

Being Welsh I took a lot of stick over my accent, especially when Charles was made Prince of Wales, I had weeks of torment and piss taking. The Scots don't like the English but will work for them and take what they can from them. They tolerate the Welsh, and on the whole I got on very well and made a lot of friends and learned a lot about human nature, and will always be grateful for the experiences I had in Scotland. I dearly loved my time there even though Anne and I had so many troubles.

The guys I worked with on the building sites were a hard drinking crew, they were from Aberdeen and Peterhead, I had my work cut out to keep up with them. Most of them lived in small touring caravans, as the work took them all over the highlands they only returned home every three weeks or so. They spent most evenings in the pub, not getting blind drunk but drinking their share, having a laugh and playing cards, I did my best to keep up but I was a beginner, I spent a lot of time in the toilet throwing up, this did cause a row or two.

One of the lads, Willy Penny, had a dog that died as a result of a dogfight. Willy was very upset, he was not married and kept himself very much to himself, he did not enter his dog in a fight it was attacked by the new in breed at that time the Rottweiler.

CROCODILE

I went into a pub one night, just to have a drink
A man was standing at the bar, looking pretty sick
I asked the landlord what was wrong, he gave a knowing wink
He lost his little dog he said, as he handed me my drink

What happed to your little dog, I asked the chap nearby?
I lost my little dog today, and tears did fill his eyes
I bet a man who stood right there, I was full of drink
That my little terrier dog, could wipe the floor with his.

He told me he had a little dog, but he's an ugly little guy
There's not a dog in all the land, would beat him in a fight
We bet our money and settled, on a field beside the pub
And the owner of the winning dog, would buy the other grub.

His dog was short, with little legs, it eyes were really sly
Its tail was short and scaly, and it swayed from side to side
He looked up at his master, and I'm sure it gave a smile
We walked out of the bar room, the snapping dogs in line.

The fight it lasted seconds, his dog it lunged at mine
And as he swallowed up my dog, he gave a toothy smile
What dog is this that eats my dog, I asked him as I cried?
Well before he had a nose job, he was a crocodile.

It's true what they say about Scots, they can drink, really drink, we in the south are mere beginners compared to them, but they are among the most generous and helpful of people I have ever met, and Aberdeen on a flag day is certainly not deserted.

When the job with this company was coming to an end, the foreman and I, a man called Gordon Rettie who insisted on being called God, were the only ones left on site. We were clearing up and doing a stocktake of equipment for return to Aberdeen, there wasn't much returned, we flogged most of the steel that was left to the local scrap merchant and tools that were left were given away for whisky or food. Any little jobs that were done on the side were 'cash in hand' jobs and there were plenty of them from tow bars to cars, to installing stainless steel pipes in distilleries. I came home with four hundred quid one week; Anne soon got rid of that.

The next job I had in Scotland was working for the M.O.D. still at RAF Kinloss this was a very relaxed base at that time and there was little or no security. I worked in the labour pool, all civilians at the beck and call of the R.A.F. I was one of about forty men, all of us had offices or buildings to look after and to keep clean, they were called sections. We were, in fact, treated as low-lives by the R.A.F., any dirty or unsavoury job, we got it.

Most of the men stayed in their own section but there were a few of us who only had morning sections and were given other jobs in the afternoon. My bosses at that time were three of the most extraordinary men I have ever met; Rodney Kelly, Bob Watson, and Wing Commander Dark. I never found out his first name. Talk about the Marx Brothers, Groucho, Chico and Harpo could not hold a candle to these. If her Majesty could have been party to some of the scams that were operated she would have us in the Tower. All sorts of gubbins, as we called it, was spirited away to various outlets, there was always a ready market for R A F gear.

Kelly, was a very down to earth kind of guy, one of the lads and would do anything to wind up Watson. Watson, on the other hand, was a very military orientated sort of man. He was in the

Seaforth Highlanders during the war and he was wounded rather badly and invalided out, much to his disappointment, he was a career soldier. Dark was always rushing around keeping the planes in the air, but relying on Kelly and Watson to keep them re-fuelled.

Bob had a twin brother Jim. They were heavily involved in the local pipe band, Jim was world champion drum major when I knew them. I still have a photo of Jim in full highland dress and bearskin holding my daughter Vicky, she was only two or three at that time. I honestly think she would have gone home with him, she fell in love with his bearskin. She cried bitterly when he handed her back to me.

When I started to work with this company of gentlemen, Bob asked me where I was from in Wales. I told him Llandrindod Wells. He seemed surprised, next day whilst at tea break Bob handed me a photograph. "Where was this taken?" He asked. I looked at the photo, it was of two men in wheelchairs being pushed along by two young girls, I must admit I went cold for a second, then I told him the photo was taken in Llandrindod Wells, in Temple Street outside the Hotel Metropole. The two girls were my Aunty Midge and my mother, then unmarried and working during the day taking wounded soldiers out for fresh air from the military hospital. I also added that I could guess what was printed on the back of the photo without looking, it said *Rushem Roberts Photographer.* He looked at me disbelieving me for a moment but I assured him my mother had got a copy of the same photo but she could not remember who the two soldiers were. They were in fact Bob and a friend whose name he could not remember, they were both recovering at the Ye Wells hospital in 1944, he was both shocked and surprised.

Small world isn't it.

One of the jobs we had to do when I worked at Kinloss was get huts ready for visiting air forces for NATO Exercises. This involved cleaning huts, making sure the bedding was laid out and a plentiful supply of toilet rolls. Wouldn't you know, no toilet rolls to be had, because of some stupid strike or other, out came the newspaper and scissors?

THE SOCK

A crises over toilet rolls, I tell you is no fun,
when your job is to ration it, two sheets to each bum.
Then what I tell you now my friends, really is no joke,
About a wing commander, my foreman and a sock.

It happened on a sunny day, when all the birds did sing,
the Foreman gave me scissors, newspaper and string.
The newspapers, I had to cut about four inches square,
Then thread them on a bit of string and hang them you know where.

All went well until you see, the paper it ran out,
And then the bloody squaddies, began to scream and shout.
We want some paper, was their cry, what a bloody caper,
My fingers they were red raw, from cutting all this paper.

So then, I said enough's enough, and refused to cut no more,
Then it happened all at once, the s—t came at the door.
Then at the dawning of a day, there came this strange command,
In front of Wing Commander Dark, I was summoned so to stand.

Into his office two men marched and stood there for inspection,
Winc'o Dark, was a stern man, we expected no redemption.
He pointed to a small box that was placed upon his desk,
He asked us each in turn to kindly this inspect.

When I looked into the box, I saw it was a sock,
Then Bob took a peep, he agreed it was a sock.
Winc'o Dark looked at both of us, and asked us each in turn,
What we made of this strange gift and what of it did learn.

I looked at him for quite a while and said I did not know,
Bob was looking straight at him, trying not to glow.
But then brave Bob spoke to him, his tone was soft and cool,
You're a very lucky man, he said there wrapping it for you.

Kelly, was a different kettle of fish, he would cut loose at anyone who annoyed him. A group of us were in the pub one night when a gang of young RAF airmen tried to push past him at the bar, one lad in particular whose language was a bit rough caught the brunt of Kelly's anger, so he put him in his place in no uncertain terms. Kelly was not a young man but he was not afraid to have a go not with his fists, but with his tongue, he knew just how to curtail any situation.

KELLY

The youth he was a surly lad
His manners they were none.
He pushed and shoved at Kelly
And swore at every one.
Kelly he was shaking
From anger and from fright,
When to the youth he turned his gaze
And spoke to him that night.

Don't swear at me you callous boy
Don't push by me again.
Your language does not impress me
Though your manners give me shame.
You're just a boy in a man's world
To you it's all a game.
The youth just looked at Kelly
And his eyes they filled with shame.

Kelly feeling better now
He made the youth look tame.
The youth turned to Kelly
And made a forward gain.
Kelly's heart skipped a beat
But he wasn't going to move
The youth's voice croaked tears filled his eyes
Forgive me I was rude.

Kelly saw the shame he caused
Said I know its hard old son.
But spare a thought for those of us
Who are old and getting on.
The youth turned round and walked away
Ashamed at what he'd done,
And Kelly just rejoined the queue
And nothing more was done.

Wee Alec was a simple minded soul who would not harm a fly; he lived in a village called Hopeman in the north of Scotland and worked with us at RAF Kinloss.

He was so inoffensive and gentle, when I knew him he was in his fifties and this job was going to see him into retirement, all be it the retirement was going to be a care home, as the family he had was prepared to put up with him while he was earning, they made it clear, he would not be tolerated when he was no longer an earner.

To this effect the RAF kept Alec on out of pity. He was, as we used to say, the village idiot. He was always immaculately turned out, clean shirt every day and always wore a tie, his shoes were always polished and his hair trimmed, we asked him one day who looked after his appearance and he told us it was the only thing he was taught by his parents, keep clean and tidy and you will always be acceptable.

Dave, my new found friend and I took a special liking to wee Alec, as we called him, and as such he was assigned to us most afternoons to look after, but I must admit to playing a few jokes at Alec's expense, nothing cruel though.

Alec was always early for tea breaks no matter where he worked he was first back to the hut for tea. His pocket watch was always seven minutes fast, why seven we never found out. I got hold of a broken pocket watch then one day at tea break I asked Alec for his watch to check the time, when he handed it to me, with the aid of Dave causing a slight diversion, I swapped his watch for the broken one, I then wrapped the broken watch in a rag and set about it with a hammer. The look on Alec's face was so shocked, he was almost in tears, the rest of the company assembled, looked on in amazement, thinking I was breaking up his watch.

I made him promise that if I put the watch back together he would never be early again, this he did and again with the help of Dave, managed to put all the broken pieces into my pocket and substitute them for his watch, which I set at the correct time. Alec was true to his word, he was never early for tea again. We don't know how lucky we are, those of us who have our health and sanity, I can't imagine how it must be to be trapped in a body that will not function or a mind that is locked into a none real world.

WEE ALEC

Don't be cruel to those of us who aren't completely there
We won't do you any harm, we just want you to care.
We are innocent in our minds, and only want to please
Don't treat us as playthings and please do not tease.
So if you see somebody who is lost in their mind
Please remember this friend, please will you be kind.

Dave McDonald was my newfound friend. He came from Stirling in the south of Scotland, everybody joked that they would not hold this against him. We had lots in common, we both liked a laugh and we both messed around with cars, and were big fans of *Monty Pythons Flying Circus*. Dave was married too young, as was I, we could both see the mistakes but were trying hard to make our marriages work, to no avail.

He had a Wolsley hornet, which was a posh mini. I had a Morris Minor, old cars but we treasured them. We were members of the RAF car club, where we spent many hours, and on reflection too many hours, but it was a way of avoiding the arguments. Anne and Dave's wife Lucy were fed up with us. This was where both our marriages really started to go wrong, we were spending more and more time at the car club away from the arguments and drink. It was our way of coping, although it was a selfish way.

In 1971 I had to go to Glasgow, as Anne's grandmother had died. Dave and I went in a hired van in order to get some furniture from her flat that was left to Anne's mother. This all took place at the same time as the local derby football match between Rangers and Celtic at Ibrox Park. We were offered tickets for stand thirteen by Dave's cousin who was a warder at Barlinnie jail, he could not go as he was on duty. I don't like football and Dave was not too keen, so we declined the offer of the tickets. On that match day stand thirteen collapsed, sixty-six people were killed and over a hundred were seriously injured. Dave and I heard the news as we were travelling back north, we stopped at the side of the road and just stared at each other in disbelief, neither of us has ever forgotten that incident. How lucky we were that day, January 2nd 1971.

The last time I visited Dave, I found that his life had been turned upside down. His wife had left him and one of his sons had committed suicide. I cried for Dave and with him, time had not been kind to him, he was a shadow of the man I had once known. No parent should have to bury their children.

I have only revisited Glasgow once since, although I believe it is now a vastly changed place from what it was in the early seventies, the gangs were rife then and violence seemed to be the norm. Frankie Vaughn went to Glasgow in a bid to end the gangland problems. He had great publicity and for a day or two normality returned to that violent city, but the gangs were soon at it again.

I was mugged in Glasgow in 1969, I had just stepped off a bus in Ibrox and was set upon for no reason at all. The police came and asked if I could identify any of them, I could not, but they bundled me into the back of the police car and drove up and down the road and when I said I thought I recognised one of the gang they jumped on him and gave him a real hiding. I said I wasn't sure if he was one of the gang, they said if he wasn't he won't be mugging anybody that night. Glasgow is a hard town.

The time I spent in Scotland I enjoyed for the greater part, the one down side was Anne's mother, she was a bitch. She did not help at all, she suffered from rheumatoid arthritis and that made her a bit crabby but she made my life hell, SHE HATED ME AND I HATED HER.

Chapter Six
BACK TO WALES

Anne and I left Scotland to try to make a fresh start back in Wales. I thought if we could get away from her mother things might get back to some sort of normality, I was wrong. Trouble has always had the habit of following me but I thought if I did not tell trouble that I was moving five hundred miles away it would give me a chance to get my family and myself straight. I said my goodbyes to Dave, this parting really upset me, he was a true friend and to lose a friend is very hard. I missed Dave for a long time and have never found another friend that I could trust as I trusted Dave.

We used the Morris Minor to get down to Wales, we only had Vicky at that time and a Red Setter dog called Dusty, who was three months old and a passenger who we christened Fred. He travelled all the way to Wales with us but he did disappear when we arrived, we all missed him.

FRED

There's a spider living in my car I see him every morning,
Hanging by his silver thread his mouth wide open yawning.
Now Fred has done a runner I don't know where he's gone,
He wasn't there this morning I bet he's fallen down.
I hope he's back tomorrow I miss him very much,
I think I'll catch some flies for him and cook them for his lunch.

It took fifteen hours to get to Wales, by the time we arrived we were all, including Dusty, in a state of sheer exhaustion but we were, as we thought, ready for a fresh start. Mother was so pleased to see us and of course Vicky now three years old got spoiled rotten. She had some imaginary friends she called them Aixi, Axo and Seedy Crump, they travelled to Wales with us so Vicky had someone to talk to and she talked all the way.

We stayed at my parent's house for a few days then started the search for a place to live. My father kept digging as to the reasons we had moved down from Scotland. Who did I upset what was I running from and were the police after me for some heinous crime? Where did I think I was going to find a place to live and a job? How long was it going to be before we moved again? The questions were endless and the old tension started to creep back. He made me feel so welcome that if it hadn't been for the fact that he worshiped Vicky and Anne, he knew nothing of her illness, and mother saying it would break her heart if she lost us again, I would have moved on.

We rented a flat under the local Christian conference centre; these people were as Christian as the Romans. One other lady who had an adjoining flat said about them, they wear their Christianity as a cloak to hide their shame, she was not wrong. What a disaster, the flat was cheap, it had to be I had not yet found work, but we took it for, as we thought, a short time.

With help from father mostly reluctantly but mother put him straight on a few facts we decorated and furnished it with what we could beg and borrow until I got a job.

The flat, had a kitchen, lounge and one bedroom, a bathroom with a gas boiler that did not work when it was windy, and the wind blew a lot. There was a small room off the kitchen which we decorated for Vicky, it was quite cosy but would only do as a temporary measure until something better came along. During winter the only heating we had was an electric fire and the gas stove, it was a slum.

The Salvation Army used to stay at the conference centre and hold jamborees until the early hours keeping everyone awake, crashing cymbals and shouting praise the Lord, had I been allowed to I would have shown a few of them how to visit the Lord but was stopped by Anne.

It wasn't long before I started a job with a Cardiff company, Turners, building an extension to the local hospital, where father was still a maintenance engineer. This did not last too long as the job was well under way when I started and I was soon out of work again so I went back to work in the butcher's shop, where I did my apprenticeship. What a mistake that was. My boss was still the arrogant bastard he always was. I found it difficult to understand the reason he was the way he was, he had been gifted the butcher's shop albeit not the best of shops but he had a good trade and sold a good product, so what made him such a bad tempered person? He had chip on his shoulder and was convinced that everyone was out to get him, one day his confidence would soar the next he would sink into depression, maybe he was a manic depressive.

I did get a lot of life experience from him, he taught me not to suffer fools gladly, but he forgot to tell me who the fools were, and too late for my own good, I turned out to be the biggest fool of all. He worked me for all I was worth, he treated me like shit, but I stayed with him, God knows why. In retrospect I felt he was the brother I never had, we did have some laughs but we had more arguments. I wasn't the only one who was cheated, conned and underpaid.

During this time another baby arrived, Hugh, I really thought that the turning point had come. I had got Anne away from her mother and she seemed to settle down, I had got a permanent job and things were on the up and up then having Hugh seemed to topple her over the edge. She was fine for the first six months but she started to drink again, not a lot to start with and I only noticed how bad it was getting when the money ran out on Mondays, as I was paid on Friday we had a week to go with nothing. I had to hold money back for rent and food. When poverty marches in love marches out.

Our marriage had reached an all time low, no matter what I

did it was not enough, the rows got so bad, I started escaping to the pub to get away, I didn't know it, but I was heading down the same path as Anne. It felt good when I was drunk and bloody awful when I sobered up, so I drunk through the day to keep on top. At one point I was on a bottle of vodka a day. I can't understand how I managed to keep my sanity, job and driving licence.

Her mother's interference followed us she was an awful woman. She could of course not interfere as we were five hundred miles away but I could feel her influence. Anne started to talk like her she was dismissive of anyone or anything that did not fall into her regime of things, she became aggressive and lazy, this was not good, her mother was starting to take over from afar. I am sure if her father knew about the situation he would have helped but again I thought I could handle it, but Anne's mother ruled him for all his good points.

The saying goes "don't speak ill of the dead," well I couldn't say anything good about her in life so I am not going to change now, she was a horror. I think the reason she hated me so much was because I have a weird sense of humour. I told a joke, she was the only one not to find it funny she thought I was taking the piss, it was not intentional, or maybe it was.

The night before Anne and I got married, my parents had travelled to Scotland for the occasion, that was an occasion in itself my father had said he never wanted to see me again after I left home but mother forced him to come to see me get married. |The mood was strained, we were sat in the pub, the Crown in Findhorn, the conversation had ceased, as it does, my mother whispered to me, asking if Anne's mother worked, well it was an opportunity not to be missed as my mother was so gullible, she would believe anything I said as long as it was whispered.

I said she had a job at the RAF camp, kick starting the aircraft, and she had to start at five in the morning. Later on in the evening when the conversation had once again died, mother desperate to start a conversation asked Anne's mother what time she had to be up for work, Anne's mother questioned the inquiry and mother told her what I had said. Anne's father burst out laughing, Betty, that was her name looked across at me and the look was to last a lifetime, she spoke more to me with that look than she did ever after, and I was hated even more from that moment on.

Anne's father on the other hand was a real gent and I felt, when Anne and I split up, that I had let him down very badly and I suffered a lot of guilt and soul searching for years. After the break up, he telephoned me, to say how sorry, he was that there could be no reconciliation, that he had not realised how much, I had to put up with because of Anne's illness. I felt even more guilty then, but he said it was the best way, staying together would have been worse, and maybe led to something more serious. I can only suppose he had been going through the same sort of problems when he discovered Anne's illness that I had been going through. Her mother, on the other hand, called me all sorts of names and probably put the family curse on me. Bloody old witch.

I knew that we would never stay together after I discovered the problems she was suffering, and I just could not cope with it, although I should have made a bigger play for Vicky and Hugh. We are all very clever in hindsight, I still think I was right, the break up had to come but thinking about it, maybe I should have tried a bit harder for Vicky and Hugh, but who knows what other problems we would have encountered on the way. Anne will always be in my thoughts, I can't hate her, but I can't love her either.

I tried to tell my parents of this problem but they dismissed it, not being drinkers, save the few whiskeys father had on a Friday at the Conservative club, he was not a conservative but the drink was cheap, they could not understand how Anne could be dinking she seemed perfectly normal to them but they had never seen her normal, she was a good actress.

My parents liked Anne, although they never came to terms with her problems. It was many years later they realised she was ill. Anne decided it was time to go back to Scotland, I could not face another upheaval so we decided to part. Boxes were packed, treasures I had collected over the years, not valuable as such but things I had saved for, were all packed away and sent to Scotland. End of marriage but not of the problems.

They were just about to hit me smack in the chops.

Tennis Skirt

Across the street from the butcher's shop was this vision in a tennis skirt. Her name was Wendy and she ran a boutique. Her husband, Gareth, was working for a local gallery as a photographer. Gareth and I became close friends and used to go shooting together, and at that time neither of us could see that our lives were going to turn inside out. Wendy and Gareth were also going through a very rough patch and Wendy and I were on a collision course.

VISION

A vision in a tennis skirt appeared to me one day,
The same time every morning at nine without delay.
She opened up her shop just across the road,
I watched her every morning, carrying her load.

She used to fumble with the key to open up the door,
Because the telephone inside was ringing off the wall.
I was ringing her you see just to see her rush,
And when she went to pick it up I hung up she got flushed.

Eventually I married her thirty years ago,
And after all the ups and downs we've given it a go.
We have a son who's smashing, and cats who sleep all day,
And I wouldn't change a single thing
for a million pounds of pay.

Wendy would come into the butcher's shop most days for something or other and we got to be good friends. I can't deny fancying her, just about everyone did, she was a cracker, (still is) but at that time I was falling deeper into the drink. A close friend noticed my decline into the world of booze and took it upon himself to get me straight, I don't know why he did this but I will be eternally grateful for his help, albeit it took a long time.

Ron, was the local milkman, he had seen what was going on so he devised a cunning plan; we would only go out on a Wednesday mostly because his day off was Thursday, and he could have a lie in bed as he got up at four every morning.

The Drovers Arms in Howey Village close to the docks was where a folk band played on Wednesday, Gareth and Wendy were involved with the folk band, so it was the chosen pub. This insured that I only got pissed one night a week and it got me closer to Wendy. He could see that I was keen on her and having seen the state of me, he made this his mission, I thought it was more mission impossible but Ron had different ideas.

Anne was still in Wales at this time but the split was final. Boxes were already packed and she was ready to go at any time so I kept out of the way as much as possible. Sleeping at friends, occasionally at my mothers and sometimes in the car when I was too drunk to get out of it. I had my shotgun taken off me by a local policeman who was sympathetic towards me as he could see what was happening; maybe he thought I was going to shoot someone or myself. I got the gun back some months later when the dust had settled.

Wendy became my best friend. We would tell each other our troubles and this seemed to make them easier to bear. For a long time the friendship remained just that, contrary to local gossip. We would walk home for lunch through the park and for this brief walk we actually felt free of our troubles and I suppose this was what led to our ultimate romance but it was a long time off.

We were both living a lie with our partners so decisions had to be made and action taken, so the splits, Wendy's and mine, came more or less at the same time. Gareth moved back to south Wales,

Anne and the children went back to Scotland, it was a few weeks before I realised I could not see my children, I must have been in a dream world, this hit me very hard. I was wracked with guilt and had it not been for Ron, Wendy, Jeremy and Nicky and Andy Davie, I would certainly have gone crazy.

Wendy's boutique went bust. Gareth had escaped the trauma by returning to south Wales, Wendy had to deal with everything herself she was very brave and stood up to everything that followed. It was not an easy time for her and the gossiping vultures were gathering on the horizon, making up what they did not know and pointing their crooked little fingers at two people who had just lost everything.

So we moved in together and fought the gossips. This as you can imagine caused a mini scandal. I fell out with my parents; they were more concerned about the disgrace to the family than anything else. My father never forgave this family scandal. He said I was weak and should have made a greater effort. He would not listen to a word against Anne, he was very fond of her. He was not prepared to listen to any excuses, he wanted control and demanded Anne and I got back together but this was never going to happen. He had lost control and this hurt his pride more than anything. In retrospect he had lost two of his grandchildren, I think this is what hurt him most. If only he had taken the time to talk, things may have been different.

Then came the problems, coming at 100 miles an hour and heading straight for us, Wendy took the brunt of this onslaught from my family. I was disgusted with them; they did not know the truth and didn't want to know. Wendy was made to feel terrible and for a number of years, she was called all sorts of names, my mother and sister would cross the street either to abuse her or ignore her, depending on how the mood took them. She took it all, it upset her a great deal and I will always admire her for the way she handled the whole episode, she stuck with me. I wanted to sort things out and tell my family that if they could not accept the situation then all was lost between us, to some extent this is what happened but Wendy said keep the door open, but it took a long time to open it fully.

I did not have any contact with my family for years; they could not be bothered to listen to me so I did not want anything to do with them. If they could not accept the events that led to my marriage breakdown without feeling sorry for themselves then I did not want any part of them. Had it not been for Wendy, I doubt that I would have ever made my peace with them.

We were together with not a stick of furniture between us. It was time to start again, despite all the problems we had faced we clicked, we put the past behind us as much as we could and got on with life, such as it was. Money had to be paid to Anne for the children so Wendy's wages paid for that, my wages such as they were paid rent, food and bills.

If I was asked to give anyone advice on marriage, it would be to see a little life before settling down, don't get taken in by the sob stories, and remember when poverty marches in, love marches out. It does not matter how much in love you think you are, when things start to go wrong they take a lot of putting right. At the end of a relationship all that is left are broken hearts and lots and lots of tears, not necessarily all yours.

I had changed jobs at this time, having fallen out with Bob Knill, and was working at another butcher's shop, a competitor, this really got under Bob's skin. David Aberley had butchers just around the corner from Bob and there was great rivalry between them, mostly because they were both full of their own self-importance, but they were only little fish in a big pool. They spent more time worrying about what everybody else was doing to see what was happening in their own lives. David had a lover, he would slope off now and again to have a grope in the office, then with renewed energy and wearing a smile a yard wide come back into the shop glowing with his own self-importance. Sadly David had no chance with his lover, she was leading him a merry dance and often confessed to me she was out for what she could get and she got a lot. David's marriage eventually broke up and a few years later his son committed suicide. This cracked David up I felt so sorry for him as his son was a very nice young man, sadly a few years later David had lost his business and he too committed suicide, what a terrible waste.

I had a meat allowance as part of my wages and continued to take my allowance after Anne had left, then one day the allowance stopped. David maintained that since I had no family to keep, the meat allowance had to stop. I continued to take the meat and he took the money out of my wages. I was arrested for theft as he maintained I was taking more than I should have. The case went to Crown Court and during the time the case took to get to court I had no income, the unemployment office would not pay me subject to the outcome of the court case. The case against me was dismissed, David Aberley was reprimanded for bringing the case to court, as what he was doing was against the law, he was not allowed to take money out of my wages without my permission and he was not allowed to cancel my meat allowance as it was part of my work contract. I was out of a job again, I was upset about this as I did enjoy working for David he had a love of music and theatre as I had, I thought we got on well, evidently not.

For a while, we lived on what I shot or caught, rabbits and trout were our staple diet. I made bread and Wendy cooked pies, using a cheap luncheon meat similar to Spam, they were delicious. I had started a driver training course on lorries and it was very hard getting to and from Newtown some twenty-seven miles away. I have Jeremy to thank for getting me to my course, he let me use his car and even paid the petrol.

All the money we had coming in was from Wendy, the dole office had suspended payments to me subject to the court findings, although I did eventually get all my money backdated with an apology.

Anne had written saying she wanted nothing more off me, either money or anything for the children she had got herself a boyfriend who was earning thousands working on the rigs and he wanted to adopt the children. There was good news and bad in one letter. To let another man adopt your children, who was he? What kind of person was he? I objected very strongly, but I was five hundred miles away with no means. I was going out of my mind but tried not to show my concern to Wendy, this was very hard.

I sought advice from a solicitor and he dealt with the whole matter, adoption was never going to be as issue. I was Vicky and Hugh's father and as long as I remained so no adoption could take place, as far as the money was concerned we continued to send it, but it was returned, so we sent no more. I felt a real heel over this, and it upset me a great deal, the extra money made a difference to us but I still felt guilty and vowed to put thing right one day. Vicky and Hugh did take his name but that was all, this I think was to save embarrassment in school. Later he showed himself in his true colours, I felt such a low life when I found out and I will never get over it. I had put my children's lives in danger and knew nothing about it until years later.

I hope, this is not the end of the story as far as Vicky and Hugh are concerned, I would very much like to get to know all about them and try to mend, the long time broken bridges. It is so difficult, to keep abreast of lost family and I try to imagine them growing up and seeing them in school.

Please, don't think that an easy time was had by me or Wendy. It was bloody hard at times, having to put up with sly innuendos and cackling witches, who always knew best. How little these people know about the hard times and thanks to friends who never turned their back and to the ones who did I hope they never have to go through the trauma we had to endure.

I am not trying to make excuses for what happened but I am asking for some degree of understanding as to what we had to go through at a very immature and sensitive time of all our lives, this goes for Anne, Vicky and Hugh, they had it a lot harder than most.

Did someone once say "life's too short to stuff a mushroom"

the name Ruth Parry comes to mind, how right she was. I have learned that you do not live to work, you work to live. Don't get tied up to an unhappy relationship, start again, it is better all round and for all concerned. Someone once said to me whilst talking about someone, who was in a particularly unhappy marriage, they would be better off hung to a tree as hung to each other.

Wendy was now working for a local firm of accountants earning a reasonable wage, the problems with the boutique were being sorted out and I had passed my lorry driving test and had started back to work. We were on the climb up and it felt good.

We had managed to move from the Christians and were renting a bungalow from Wendy's boss, the name of the bungalow was Brynonnen, in the village of Penybont just outside Llandrindod Wells. It was great, we had a huge garden and we grew a lot of vegetables, no green leaf, we had a large garage, a lawn and a lake behind us where Canada geese used to nest, all out in the country peace and quiet, away from the stares of Llandrindod and all its witches and gossips. Our neighbours at this time were a lovely couple Dr. and Mrs Fraser, Hugh and Marjory, they were very kind to us and gave us veg out of their garden and advise on how to grow our own, life was getting better. No more family to cause us any problems.

Because of the break up of our marriages the Wednesday night at the Drovers was short of a guitar player. Gareth had gone so we became involved with a very talented musician Andrew Davies. Andy could sing and play anything so the three of us started a folk club at the Llanarch Hotel, after the break up we did not feel right going to the Drovers Arms, so we changed pubs this was our new local pub, we called ourselves Barleycorn, both the club and us were a great success.

During the time of the folk club we made friends with a guy called Ian Ball he was a religious instruction teacher and an all round nice chap. His wife Jackie is a real country style girl with a wicked sense of humour and such a laid back charm that would have you fawning at her feet, if she so desired. Ian was so enthusiastic about every thing he took on. He was also a very funny folk club performer, relating such tales as *The Dragon of Wantly* with such enthusiasm as to having the audience literally falling down laughing uncontrollably.

Ian wanted to take up shooting, as he said it may supplement the table from time to time, so I was enlisted to help get him his gun licence and teach him how to shoot. Ian acquired his licence and a single barrel 12 bore shotgun and set off to kill anything he could eat. After a few months we, that is Wendy and I, had an invitation to join a shoot, on Llangunllo hill, near Knighton, in mid Wales. We accepted the invitation, knowing we would meet some very interesting people from all walks of life and get fed into the bargain, we were not disappointed.

We met a horse whisper, called Pete who was Mexican, and he really did whisper to horses. His training methods were amazing, he could go into a field with a totally unbroken horse and in a few hours he would be riding it. What a fantastic guy. Also in the company were two people who were into battle re-enactment. English civil war, all that sort of thing, they were going to shoot with the weapons that were used in the civil war. Charles, who was a very flamboyant sort of chap from Yorkshire, and was a proof reader for a big publishing company, had a flintlock muzzle-loading gun about 20 bore calibre, a very fine piece.

Dave, another Yorkshire man, more down to earth than Charles, had a matchlock, this was six feet long and had to be rested on a forked stick to fire, again muzzle loading, but had to be fired by means of a piece of smouldering rope which was flashed against the powder pan which fired the gun.

So, picture the scene, me with a double barrel 12 bore, Wendy single barrel 12 bore, Ian single barrel 12 bore, Charles a 20 bore flintlock, and Dave a matchlock of dubious bore that had to be fired with the aid of a piece of burning rope and a large forked stick, two dogs and several hangers on to carry the days trophies home. Hip flasks were in abundance, along with packed lunches of cheese, bread and apples. If the devil should have cast his net that day.... I gave instructions to the assembled company, no walking in line astern and no loaded guns to be carried uphill.

What a day it turned out to be, one rabbit shot and a funeral. The only rabbit shot was buried with full military honours and the assembled company returned home with saddened hearts.

POOR BUN

The morning broke a misty cool September day
When all the hunters came outside to play.
With lunches packed and dogs so keen
We set out on the hunt to see what can be seen.

Peasants are the favourite or a duck or two
And if a rabbit should show itself he would end up in a stew.
The dogs were searching hedgerows and sniffing all around
Hunters watched with baited breath scanning all around.

Then all at once a mighty bang and a great big puff of smoke
The matchlock had been fired at a rabbit running round.
Not a mark was on the rabbit as he took off up the track
But the hunter with the matchlock was lying on his back.

We laughed so much at this event and at his blackened face
As he pulled himself together to save a bit of grace.
Then as we laughed the flintlock sent a loud resound
And the rabbit that he shot at tumbled to the ground.

The party it fell silent at this creature's fast demise
And as we looked upon its corpse tears they filled our eyes
We buried that poor rabbit with honours duly read
And trundled off back home with pity in our head.

We never shot another thing the guns were put away
No more killing would we do on that awful day.
We never forgot that little bun and drank to his demise
So never kill just for fun that is our advice.

~*~

A few weeks later, we were at a folk festival, in Bromyard, a familiar face came walking towards us, together with another familiar face on crutches. Charles, was on crutches accompanied by Ian, it transpired that Charles, on another hunting trip, had inadvertently double loaded his flintlock, the barrel had split in two, knocking him to the ground, with such force he had broken his leg, fractured his ribs and badly bruised his face where the stock of the gun had whacked him. He had powder burns on his face and looked very sorry for himself he was in a very poor state, but it did not interfere with his enjoyment of the folk festival, he later vowed to restore the gun and hang it on the mantelpiece. I don't know if he ever did as the promise was made under the influence of several pints of very strong real ale.

Ian was ordained as a minister of the church and his ordination was at Hereford Cathedral we were invited, it was such a wonderful day for Ian and his family. After the ceremony Ian and I embraced like brothers, he was so pleased we had made the journey to witness his great day, I would not have missed it for anything we were very close. A few tears were shed that day and a few drinks taken in celebration. The next time I was to see Ian was at Jeremy's funeral, he had suffered a nervous breakdown but I am glad to say he was on the long road to recovery.

I went to work for Harry at R & B Transport as a lorry driver. I was driving an old Bedford T.K. tipper I thought it was brilliant, my first lorry driving job. The boss or should I say one of the bosses Harry Rice was a tight fisted man, he would stand over us as we put oil and diesel in the lorry, to make sure we didn't spill any or put too much in. Wages were paid to the halfpenny and overtime was scrupulously checked, but for all his faults, he laughed at my jokes and shouted at me when I did things wrong, but he paid for my class one licence. Thanks Harry. Harry's mum was the boss despite Harry's attempts to take over she remained *the* boss.

HARRY'S MUM

Harry was a tight old git,
to part with money gave him a fit
Overtime he rarely paid,
he counted his pennies every day,
Lorries though they were the best,
painted up in real fine dress.
No battle scars on Harry's trucks,
for if there was he'd give you f...k
His mother though, she was the boss,
always causing such a fuss.

Saying she was always ill,
and nothing to leave him in her will
Don't die on a weekend, he would say,
for the men will have to have a day
To put you deep into the ground,
will surly cost a pretty pound
A fish pool in the garden big,
when work was short we did dig
Piranhas he would breed in it,
to eat up mother and save a quid.

The job finished with Harry, the council contract he had finished putting a few of us out of work. I was sorry to leave but I moved on to earn more money.

Wendy and I were trying to buy Brynonnen but money was really tight, so we had to cut out lots of things like going to the pub and of course the folk club, we had managed to save £750.00 for the deposit on Brynonnen.

Wendy's boss, a guy called John Bean, was a senior partner in a firm called Moor Scott & Co, Accountants. He was very good to Wendy, I think he fancied her although his wife kept him on a very short leash he was known to stray now and again.

Anyway we needed £1000 and he had put a time limit on us to raise the cash, we were struggling, it was 1974 and wages, were not too good. Together we were not earning that much so we started to panic. I had started work in an abattoir in Builth Wells as a driver/loader and as such worked nights taking loads to Smithfield market in London so I was away two or three nights a week, this meant I slept through the day. Wendy worked through the day so as she was coming home I was going to work, we saw little of each other for a while but we desperately wanted to buy this bungalow it was exactly what we wanted and we had fallen in love with the village and the people, so the extra money came in very handy.

Enter Fred Cross

Wendy's father had been killed in 1966 in a shipping accident in New York. Fred Cross had made it his business to keep his eye on her family and take care of them, as if her father was still alive. Wendy's mum contacted Fred to see if there was anything he could do to help us. We were summoned to London to an office just behind Fleet street, the British Steam Navigation and Coal Company, which I believe was a subsidiary owned by Fred, but part of a much larger shipping company called Vlassof or something similar, anyway there we were, in this office block staring across the desk at this huge man who was like a big soft bear, his smile was complimented by almost perfect teeth and for a man of seventy years was surprising. We later found out they had all been capped, because he had worn his own out.

After the initial introduction and his very strong handshake followed a preliminary chat about how Wendy's mum was and so forth. He asked if we had eaten, we could hardly afford the petrol to get to London, food was a luxury we were starving. We were taken to lunch at his club, what an experience, I had never been to such a smart place, we felt very special. Fred was tipping waiters ten pounds a time, I almost jumped up and grabbed a tea towel and started waiting myself! We talked through lunch about work and prospects of which I had none except to keep working, but he kept saying he was so glad that Wendy had grown up into such a determined woman and he was sure we were going to be all right.

After a lunch, that would have normally fed both Wendy and I for a week, we were taken back to Fred's office, where he presented us with a cheque for the £250 00 we were short to make our deposit. This was just a loan, he emphasised 'a loan', we accepted and we were so happy, to celebrate we went to look around *Harrods*, we spent our last pound on some kippers, of all things, just to get the shopping bag, what a pair of fools, but it made us feel good, we were on top of the world, we still think if it feels good it must be right. The kippers were pretty good as well. Wendy and I got married on December the 18th 1976 that felt right, our best man was Andrew Davies he forgot the camera so no record of the occasion exists.

A few years later when our son Kirk was born, Fred sent us a really nice letter, congratulating us on the birth of our son, and in the letter he said the £250.00 was to be given to Kirk as a present, what a man he was.

We bought Brynonnen, our own home, my family were livid, trouble was on the horizon again had it not been for Wendy's intervention I am sure World War Three would certainly have broken out.

Chapter Seven

During the period of buying Brynonnen and before Kirk was born or even thought of another shock came our way. Anne had arrived with Vicky and Hugh, two baby daughters and a Labrador dog, how she had managed to get them all down from Scotland was nothing short of a miracle. She was so drunk she could hardly stand, she wanted to leave Vicky and Hugh with us for a time until she said she got her life back on track. Vicky and Hugh were totally confused, they were tired and hungry, and not too clean. My parents insisted that they should stay with them.

Wendy and I were working full time, so this arrangement was reluctantly agreed upon there was no other way around the situation. Anne stayed a couple of days with my parents, my mother was shocked at the state of her and finally realised the reasons for our divorce. She wanted to help Anne and she insisted she stay for longer so she stayed for a week all the time, unknown to mother, drinking secretly.

Whilst she was in Llandrindod she took my sister's children and her babies for a walk to the local lake. Vicky and Hugh stayed with mother, she had been gone some hours when she was found unconscious with an empty whisky bottle beside her and the children crying and bewildered Thankfully she was found by a local man John (Tubby) Price he looked after them until mother collected them, thankfully they came to no harm. Next day Anne started off back to the highlands, we didn't hear from her for a whole year. She never phoned or contacted any of us. Vicky and Hugh went through a period of depression but as time went on they cheered up and even enjoyed going to school. They both wanted to stay permanently with my parents in Wales.

During this time I went to Hereford family court to try and get permanent custody of them, but Scottish law being what it is, I had no chance at all. Then one day out of the blue Anne turned up with husband Charles and took them away again. Had I known then the reason for her depositing Vicky and Hugh she would never have taken them back. I was not to see them again for seventeen years. During those years I was denied all access to them, I would get the occasional postcard but no more. After having them close for a year it was once again very hard to come to terms with the fact that they had gone.

Wendy was pregnant when they went back to Scotland and this somehow took the sting out of my despair. We were busy getting a room at Brynonnen ready for our new arrival, the walls had to be plaster boarded and all paintwork renewed, there was a cot to buy as well as all sorts of sundries for a nursery, we looked forward to the event and poor Wendy grew at an alarming rate and had to stop working. She was a geriatric mother as she was thirty when Kirk was born and taken to Hereford hospital some forty miles away to be delivered.

Kirk arrived on the 19th September 1980, a new family had begun we were so proud this was the new start we had been hoping for although our new start came with a nasty sting in the tail. Kirk was born with a heart defect and had to undergo several operations, these operations were performed in the Birmingham Children's Hospital. This was a traumatic time for both of us and Kirk, he was so small and helpless and totally in the hands of the doctors and nurses who gave him so much care and attention, we were constantly on the road to Birmingham.

During this time I was working for Bob Knill again, he was very understanding, giving me time off and letting me book petrol on his account to help me out. He got paid back, but I will always be grateful to him for this despite all the bad times we had, he did help me then. Thank you Bob.

I was on better terms with my family until one day when I had just got back from Birmingham. I was totally exhausted, all I wanted was a shower and a cup of tea that did not taste of hospital. Kirk had just had his first operation and Wendy had stayed in Birmingham with him where she spent a few very uncomfortable nights sleeping on two chairs pushed together. I had to return home in order to feed the dogs, we had two at that time, Dusty and her pup Winston.

My father telephoned me to ask how the 'boy' was getting on. He couldn't even call Kirk by name, he was still stinging. I suppose he did not consider Kirk a grandson, he was very distant and it transpired that mother had told him to ring rather than ring on his own accord which he would never do. I told him he had just had an operation on his heart and Wendy was staying in the hospital with him as there was a fear things may not go as planned. He asked if he could help with anything, I said I could do with a loan of a hundred pounds, just to help with travelling expenses I assured him he would be repaid as soon as I got back on my feet. The line went quiet for a while I thought he had hung up then he said he would gladly help, if he had the money, but things were a bit tight at the moment so he could not, I understood and said no more.

A couple of days later I was serving a man in the butcher's shop, I had been in school with him and he now worked as a car salesman, we were chatting away when he asked what I thought of my father's new car.

'What car?' I asked.

He told me that he had picked it up that morning.

'On the HP?' I asked jokingly.

'No, he paid cash for it.'

I went ballistic. I don't remember what I said to my father, I was more concerned how I was going to tell Wendy; I was totally gutted at this revelation. I did not speak to my family for eight years and again had it not been for Wendy I would never have spoken to them again. I realised at that point that I would never hold my family close to me again. I would tolerate them and help if the need was desperate but only if it were desperate. I can't put into words what I felt at that time and how it affected my relationship with my family.

Kirk got through all his operations although he did give us cause for a lot of concern. I'm glad to say, he is fit and well, thanks to the skill and wonderful care of the surgeons and nurses at the Children's Hospital in Birmingham. He has grown up into a very nice, kind, young man.

He attended University College London, where he studied archaeology and forensics. He worked so hard to get there sacrificing his free time in order to pass the exams he has made us so proud.

During his four years in university he lived in Camden, north London, we visited as often as we dared. We did not want to interfere in his life too much or was it that each time we saw where he lived we wanted to bring him home. I wanted him home but was guided by Wendy once more and did not interfere, 'he has to get on with life', she said amid sobs and tears. I know the first time we left him in the halls of the university we both shed a tear but he survived. We are so proud of him and look forward to seeing which direction his studies may take him. I wish I had given him more time when he was a child but I was so busy trying to survive, we can all see what we should have done in hindsight. His name 'Kirk' is a proud name, it belongs to someone who will not suffer fools gladly and he knows who they are, not like his old man.

FOR KIRK

Independence is a wondrous thing
It truly makes your young heart sing
Just do what you want in life
As long as you don't cause other's strife.
Remember son I'm always here
To lend a sympathetic ear
And give a quid if that's all it takes
To get yourself from place to place.

We had to furnish Brynonnen so we went to auctions and second-hand stores. We needed a carpet so we went to see a local dealer, she was at one time, I think of gipsy origin but her family had settled in town during the First World War and she was considered to be something of a Gipsy Queen by whoever came to know her. She was a darling, she would sell anything from scrap metal to gold sovereigns and always managed to make a profit. The whole family had a speech impediment, every member of the family was afflicted, aunties, uncles, children all had a stutter. The carpet she showed us had a huge hole in the centre but not to be done out of a sale she told us to put a table in the centre and no one would notice, we declined but were invited in for a cup of tea before leaving, probably in the hope of selling something else. On entering the house we could not help but see a large cage with an African grey parrot, the parrot also talked with a stutter.

PARROT

We went to buy a carpet, second hand, from this gipsy queen
We were assured by her son it was the best that we would see.
He said come down to see it, I'm sure you'll be impressed
My mum will do the dealing, at that she is the best.

Down we went to see it, no thoughts of doubt we uttered
Then saw the gipsy lady and listened to her stutter.
'Th...the very b...best of q...quality,
I'm s...sure you w...will agree'
As she rolled out this carpet, for both of us to see.

She rolled the carpet some way out, for us to take a peek
But we were not too sure of it, the pattern so to speak.
We'd like to see it all rolled out, for to get the size
But as she rolled it fully out, a hole it caught our eyes.

The hole was in the middle, it showed up really well
She stuttered 'p...put a t...table over it, nobody will t...tell'.

We looked at the carpet, spread across the ground
And said we think we'll leave it, we'll have a look around.

No offence was taken, the carpet was rolled away
She asked us in for a cup of tea, before we went away.
Sat upon the dresser, in a brass cage big and bold
Was this huge parrot, colours green, red and gold.
'His n…name is A…Albert,
we've h…had him tw…twenty years
He talks as w…well and t…tells jokes, he really is a dear.'
We looked in at the parrot, but not a sound he uttered
But as we drank our cup of tea, he talked with a stutter.

He really could tell a joke, and talked so fast and clear
But stuttered out his every word, it was so plain to hear.
We made our exit pretty quick, and bid them all farewell
And said no one will believe us when this tale we tell.

Just to add a note the parrot had a lamb chop for his tea every day.

We furnished Brynonnen and were pleased with the result we had settled down and were content with our lot. A new cooperative Welsh Quality Lamb was starting up in Builth Wells and I went to work for them as a loader/driver, the job was in an abattoir. My job was to load lorries and drive to Smithfield meat market at night, not much of a job, but it helped to keep the wolf from the door and we got a lot of cheap meat. The job was hard and I worked long hours, sometimes eighteen, or twenty hours a day, normal in that job.

At the abattoir, there was a pay clerk named Kath she was so stubborn and full of her own self-importance, she caused the workforce to revolt on more than one occasion, she was not popular. Revenge is a dish best served cold, as the saying goes, and the revenge was played out in such a way, that it changed Kath into a more understanding person. One of her little bits of power was to hold back the pay until the last minute, so if there were any queries, she would not deal with them until the following week. This caused real problems as you can imagine, so a plan was hatched to bring her to heel, this was a cruel trick but Kath was a more understanding person after. It involved a duck, the duck was not hurt in any way but what a way to tame the ogre.

DUCK A LOO

When working as a loader, a woman paid our wage
She was a real old dragon, and well set in her ways.
The pay should be ready, for one o'clock you see
For the wives to collect, to get the men their tea.

She never made a secret of the hate she held for us
I think she would have liked to have been a conductor on a bus.
So she could take us far away and in her wicked mind
Throw all of us off her bus and leave us all behind.

She used to get the wages wrong and bonuses not pay
When we went up to her with the intention to complain
Her answer it would always be, this is not the way
To get upon her good side, we should ask and not complain.

Each morning as she parked her bike and chained it to her door
The men would fix her with a gaze, as she stomped across the floor
He eyes fixed, her glare stitched, her head it never moved.
As she made her way, kettle in hand, to the ladies loo.

One morning in the autumn as the sun was shining bright
She cycled up to her door and chained up her old bike
The air was tense, as all the men stared at her that day
And watched her going to the loo and wait to hear the fray.

As the loo door it did close, the tension it was great
The screams that followed Kath, running for her mate.

A duck you see, fit and well, was waiting in the loo
And as she lifted up the lid, it gave her quite a shoo.

Each morning now she parks her bike and shouts to us hello
The wages they are never late and her door is never closed.
We all agree there is no doubt that Kath she is the best
But if she's ever bad again, there's a mouse for down her vest..

I worked with two men, I was in school with, or should I say we attended the same school at slightly different times, but had been friends for years. John was unmarried and always seemed to be a bit rough. He was loud and very brash but under the rough exterior he was a very shy and gentle person. John was a diesel fitter by trade and a very clever man, if he could not buy a part he would make it. His biggest problem was he suffered from depression and headaches, this made him nervous and irritable. He would sink into deep moods and ignore everyone when a mood took over, something like Churchill's black dog moods as they were known. It was his way of working through them, then as fast as his mood came so it went and he was once again himself laughing and joking. After a while these attacks became less and life at last seemed be going in the right direction for him. He had met a soul mate, one who he could confide in, Shelia, she knew what black dog moods were like and knew how to treat them.

MY MATE JOHN

John, he was a nervous chap
All lifes troubles were in his lap
Of worries he had every one
And most of those were other's ones.

And then one day he went insane
Never it seemed to worry again
But this alas was not the end
His troubled mind it would not end.

In his room by day and night
His mind was in a constant fight
His eyes would flash his head it ached
But still his troubles he'd debate.

The nurses they all talked to John
He really is a clever one
From topics such as cars and planes
To subjects that would tax your brain.

John had the answer in his mind
But life to him was such a bind
They tried him on some tablets first
But for John they did not work.

They put him in a padded cell
But this move did him no well
Until one morning clear and bright
John's eyes took on a shining light.

His troubles now they near the end
All the people are now his friends
He sits and talks to many now
And troubled lines don't mark his brow.

For he woke up one morning bright
And told us of a big bright light
This light he says was hot and red
And seemed to shine inside his head

He doesn't worry any more
Nor does he stamp upon the floor
No on knows just what John saw
But now the lock is off his door.

He walks again his head held high
A lady walking at his side
The light now shining in his eyes
Is a light for the lady at his side?
They always walk together now
No lines of worry on their brow

Dave was a different person altogether, a farmer and a happy man who loved life, he worked as a loader. He had lost the thumb on his left hand, it happened when he was a child, he got it caught in a piece of farm machinery called a chaff cutter. He managed fine without it, he was immensely strong, but he was a gentle giant and would do anything to help anybody. He owned a farm and took the job as loader to supplement the farm. I went to the farm one year to help with sheep shearing, what a mistake that was! I was the catcher, this meant I caught the sheep and took them to the Shearer. Anybody who thinks farming is a simple life should try shearing, I was completely knackered for days. After the shearing came the tea, I have never seen a table laid out like it, there was ham, pies, cheese, bread, salad, almost everything you could imagine was laid on the table along with cider or beer and gallons of tea. The saying, 'to eat like a farmer' is right. I was told that Dave, at one time for a bet, had sat down and eaten a seven-pound tin of corned beef. Judging by the size of him, I can well believe it.

There was a stream running through his land and it was a real treat, to go out in the winter nights and poach a salmon or two, we were never greedy, it was one for the pot. What a thrill to wade into the water with a torch and a gaff, a stick with a large hook attached, then shine the torch onto a salmon and mesmerise it then gaff it. Salmon always tasted better when poached. When we worked together the job always ended up as a competition, no guesses as to who always won.

ALL FINGERS

The gang was at a tea break the work was very hard
And as had become the custom, they were swapping silly yarns
When all at once the door was knocked,
and in the frame we saw
A gentle giant of a man, asking was this the loader's door?

I answered yes and asked him in and offered him some tea
No milk he said and looked around to find himself a seat
I gave him tea and noticed, part of him was gone
But made no mention of it, for fear that it was wrong.

We sat awhile and talked about the work and what to do
Then the giant whose name was Dave, said what am I to do
You'll work with me I told him and instantly I felt
I had a friend in whom to trust, a farmer and a gent.

When work commenced I noticed, the hand that had no thumb
Not wishing to offend him, I offered comments none
The weeks went by the job went on, mostly into night
Stories to be told, were getting very light.

But on one night I commented about the missing thumb
Dave's eyes lit up and then he smiled, what's taken you so long?
I said that I was worried, in case offence he took
Then he smiled, held out his hand for every one to look.

It happened when I was small, playing in the yard
A chaff cutter wheel was turning and I gave it such a stab
The wheel it kept on turning, along with my poor thumb
And in those days as you all know, not much could be done.

There were some things I could not do, that gave me so much grief
But practise every evening and I could do them all with ease
The first were shirt cuff buttons, they really were a beast

But two fingers and my teeth I did them up with ease.

In later life, I used to watch people rolling fags
I tried this for a long time, but could not get a drag
But in good time I also learned, one handed this to do.
But then I cut my other thumb, I leave the rest to you.

When you have grown up in a farming community, even though you are not a farmer yourself, you do tend to get involved with the people who are. I was always assured a welcome at the country pub I used as my local, as I went to school with the now landlord. The pub was a favourite haunt of local farmers, a meeting place for several committees of one sort or another. A typical country pub on the edge of a small but well catered for village, a small store and post office, a well run market, which operated on the third Wednesday of each month. Inside a welcoming atmosphere, open fireplace, a little smoky in a strong wind but warm and friendly.

Hunting memorabilia hung on the walls, pictures of country scenes, all prints but they lent a feeling of tradition. There were exposed beams on the ceiling with hooks to hang bacon sides still in evidence, as the pub had long ago been a farmhouse. A well-stocked bar a good variety of beers, although cider was the preferred drink with the locals. The pub was more of a community centre. On Mondays; darts, Tuesday; pool, Wednesday; farmers' wives who would organise the year's events for the local Women's Institute and the forthcoming agricultural shows. Thursday was quiet. Friday was the Young Farmers' Club, a bit riotous so we kept away. Young farmers have a unique way of letting their hair down. Saturday was a social evening, no meetings or committees just friendly banter among the locals. Sunday was quiet as it was Sunday. Church or chapel in the morning, or if you were busy then you attended in the evening, so the pub was out for most locals, just the occasional passing trade.

One particular Saturday early in March, the clocks had not yet changed, the nights were still cold and dark. It was around nine in the evening and I was having a drink and chat with half a dozen or so, sitting around the fire telling tales when the door burst open with such force everyone stopped talking and looked around to see who had burst in with such urgency. The door slammed shut, enter Tom Williams who he was not renowned for his speed or his spending power. Leaning on the bar, getting his breath, he ordered a double whisky, Tom had never had a double of anything in his life unless of course someone else was paying. If Tom ordered this amount of whisky something was wrong, this was not the Tom we knew. The landlord put the drink in front of him, looking across at us and winking towards Tom who took the glass in both hands and gulped it down in one swallow, coughing at its strength, then motioned to the optic for a refill. We stared in amazement, we knew Tom and had never seen him drink strong liquor before. Something must have happened to make him act in such a way.

The bar fell silent, Tom seemed to gain some composure, his eyes flashed about the room searching, then seeing the company around the fireplace, made a move towards us, still clutching his second drink in a very shaky hand.

Breaking the silence Jack Thomas, a long time friend of Tom's asked.

"What is the matter old son? You look like you've seen a ghost."

Tom stared. "I have Jack, I bloody well have, well not so much seen as heard."

He sank into a seat beside the fire and we looked at each other.

Although this was a farming community and a religious one, all had the view that if you believed in God then you believed in the devil, so seeing a ghost stirred their interest.

"Come on old son..." Jack called everyone old son, probably because it was easier than trying to remember names, he called all women darling, or as he spoke darlin,

"Tell us what did thee see?"

Tom took a sip of his drink, he did not gulp it down, probably now realising its strength, then ordered a pint of cider.

"They won't mix." Another member of the company spoke, "You'll be sick as a pig, drinking cider on top of that stuff."

Tom looked at the man who'd spoken, he smiled inwardly, he could remember carrying him home on many occasions when they were younger and telling him not to mix his drinks.

Tom now gathering his senses looked around, eyes still glazed. It is a fact that when you have had a shock you may look at things but you do not really see them, not until the shock has worn off, this was now happening to Tom. He greeted each of us in turn.

All were farmers except me, very hard working no nonsense men who worked in all weathers, all had the leathery completion, which only comes from working outdoors. All ears were now poised as to what tale Tom was about to relate. The landlord pulled up a chair, eager to hear the tale Tom was about to tell. The landlord had taken over the pub from his father and his father before him. He was as much a part of the community as anyone, he helped out at harvest and shearing, he loved the countryside and was as much involved as anyone could be in preserving it and had gone to great lengths to make the pub as much of a home to the locals as he could.

Tom took a sip from his cider then reached into his pocket and took out an old battered tin. The tin was older than Tom, he had been left it by his grandfather, he treasured it, and carried it everywhere, his wife used to say if he ever got lost look for the tin and Tom would be attached to it. He opened it and proceeded to make himself a cigarette, after licking the paper and lighting it, he took a long draw, again coughing slightly as he did, all ears and eyes were now on Tom.

He spoke, his voice shaking. He was clearly frightened, even though he was among friends.

"I was coming down the road on my bike." (Tom always rode an old bicycle to the pub, mainly because he needed something to lean on, when going home, he did tend to take a bit too much drink on Saturdays.) "I was passing Billy's yard, I heard this noise, a sort of snuffling, snorting noise coming from the hedgerow by the yard."

Billy's yard was a timber yard, used by the Forestry Commission to process and ship the hundreds of tons of trees that were felled in the area. The Forestry Commission had thousands of acres of trees and had taken over Billy's yard as grading yard. Trucks were loaded with the timber of various sizes then shipped to wherever it was to be processed into usable timber or paper mulch.

Tom continued taking another sip of his drink.

"I stopped and listened but heard nothing, then I started to move again, the noise started again, so I stopped and the noise stopped."

"What did you see?" Asked Jack.

"I didn't see anything but every time I moved whatever it was moved and made a groaning noise."

"It's Sam!"

The voice belonged to the oldest member of the company. Puffing on his pipe, he looked to the ceiling as if to get inspiration. Ned had farmed the property above Billy's yard all his life and well remembered the tragedy that had taken place there years before. A load of timber had fallen off the side of a lorry and crushed a local worker. His name was Sam Sumere. Sam was not a local, he came from foreign parts, no one knew exactly where, it was rumoured he had come from Poland at the end of the war, he was good at fixing watches and clocks, but he did not mix well, only with a few, he was a very private man. Sam had not died instantly, he suffered crush injuries and was in much pain and he swore and cursed the timber yard saying he would come back and haunt it.

"Don't be dull Ned," answered Tom, "he can't come back can he?"

Ned knocked his pipe out on the fireplace causing sparks to fly, well he always said he would. Tom looked at all sat at the fire and slumped back in his seat.

"What did you see?" We asked.

Tom looked around the room again.

"Nothing it was too dark but he was there I know it was him he was now convinced Sam had returned and looked for another drink.

"Well let's go and find out," said the Landlord.

The bravery of those who ventured out that night would have made Churchill proud. The pub emptied, all but the Landlord's wife joined the throng, marching up the road towards Billy's Yard.

Billy Tomlins used to own Billy's Yard. The Forestry Commission bought it from him when he retired, but it would always be known as Billy's Yard. It had been, in its time, was as much of a meeting place for the locals as the pub. Billy used to sell all sorts, second hand farm implements, wooden seats, tables, it was a farmers' shop he sold paraffin and T.V.O. tractor vehicle oil to run older tractors and stationary engines that used to run shearing machines and a small but efficient blacksmith shop. In fact, Billy sold just about everything, a real Aladdin's cave. He had suffered ill health for a few years so when the screws as he called his rheumatism had forced his retirement, he moved away to the coast where his daughter had a bed and breakfast hotel.

As the brave fearless occupants of the pub rushed out into the gloom, the cold night air took their breath away. The night was cold but on they went, towards Billy's yard and the ghost. Each electing to take the lead in the march forward until they came closer to their destination, then the pace slowed and each wished they had drunk a whisky before venturing out into the dark uninviting night. What would happen if they did encounter a ghost? How were they going to deal with it? Someone said go and get the vicar. He would exercise it.

"Don't be daft," said Ned, "you can't take it for a walk you silly bugger."

A muffled laugh drifted through the company, Tom whispered.

"You *exorcise* a ghost and send him back where it came from, anyway the vicar wouldn't be best pleased to be dragged out here this time of night."

Just as they approached the spot where Tom had heard the ghost they stopped to take stock of the situation. Tall hedgerows lined the road and it was hard to see through the gloom, nobody had thought to bring a torch. The plan was to walk on very quietly and see if they could surprise whatever was there, if, anything was there at all. They crept forward inching ever closer to the spot, each pushing the one in front, someone sneezed, all jumped with fright, then amid calls for hush, stood still and listened. Nothing was heard.

"Tom," Jack whispered, "go forward gently see if it comes out."

"Why me?" Asked Tom.

"Because it's your bloody ghost."

Tom looked pale, even in the darkness he looked pale, he felt his legs go weak, they refused to move, he was stuck to the spot.

"I can't bloody well move," he whispered.

It seemed like hours until a voice said very softly but firmly. "If you don't move I'll put my boot in your arse."

Tom moved forward.

Just then they all heard it, moving, groaning, snuffling in the undergrowth. Tom stopped, it stopped. Tom moved, it moved. At this Tom took fright and made to get away but was held on to by Ned.

Everyone froze, then Ned let go of Tom and hurled himself through the hedge, to where the noise was coming from, shouting at the top of his voice, more out of fear than bravery. "Let's have you, you bugger come on out!"

There was a crash, a howl from Ned, then a dragging sound. Ned cried for help, several others dived through the hedge, I didn't; I'm no hero. There followed a great laugh. They reappeared dragging a calf, it was more frightened of us than we were of it, although five minuets before it was not so, the animal was lost it would follow any sound looking for its mother. After releasing the calf safely into a nearby field all eyes were on Tom.

Tom in turn did not know where to look, he was so embarrassed by the whole affair, all he could do was to apologise and offer everyone drinks back at the pub. The walk back was full of laughter and poking fun at Tom who could not hide his embarrassment.

Tom meets everyone at the pub every Saturday night, as usual he still peddles his bike down the road but he peddles very fast past Billy's Yard, still not fully believing that it was just a calf that frightened him so much.

THE GHOST OF BILLY'S YARD

The fire was bright, the night was dark
as the lad burst through the door
His face was drawn, his hands they shook,
as he rushed up to the bar
"A drink, please John, a whisky please, I've had a nasty scare."
He took the drink down in a gulp and stumbled to a chair.

"A scare," The locals asked the lad,
"when was this and where?"
The lad then downed another drink and stuttered, "out there."
The locals were all standing round
as the lad's voice quaked with fear
And as the lad he told his tale the bar was full of ears.

"I came out from the lane, you know leading from the farm
I pushed the bike up the hill and was passing Billy's yard
I thought I heard a scuffling, from behind the shed
I stopped and looked and listened, but not a sound I heard.

I started down the road again and then I heard it more
Running after me it was, of that I'm pretty sure
I stopped the bike and called to it, 'come out if you dare'
But not a movement did I see, just the whisper of the air."

By then a crowd had gathered round, to see about the fuss
The lad was feeling better now and wasn't such a mess
Then old Ned with icy voice, spoke out,
"I now what you did hear
It's old Sam's ghost that's chasing you, I'll bet a pint of beer."

"What's that you say," they questioned,
"you mean old Sam Sumere?"
"That's him," said Ned, "I think he's back
and I knew he would appear.
Billy's yard is where he died, I remember it right good
Crushed, he was, into the ground, by twenty tons of wood."

The lad by now had drunk a lot and courage filled his veins
"I'm going out to find old Sam, and make him feel ashamed."
"Hang on young lad, don't be haste, we'll come along in case."
So out into the cold night air a dozen, men did race

The room was suddenly empty now, the crowd it was no more
The bar it lost its fiery heat, as they left an open door
They walked up to the place where the lad had heard the noise
They listened for the slightest sound, while peering into the void.

"It won't move until we do," the lad was heard to say
So all at once the crowd moved on, quiet as the grave.
They stopped again and listened and not a sound they heard
They called out, 'is that you old Sam', but came back not a word.

They moved once more, then so did it, they really took a fright
What can it be but old Sam, stalking through the night.
Just then a mighty sound was heard, just as death should sound
It seemed to tear the very air, and shake the very ground.

"That's it! I've had enough," Ned was heard to swear
He turned towards the noise and hurtled through the air.
"Come out you ghost and say your bit, this doesn't make us laugh."
He grasped at something solid and gave a mighty gasp.

The rest stood back, then they fought
and pulled it from the gloom
The lad stood back and watched the fray,
not knowing what to do.

Then all at once the hedgerow broke,
and a calf came galloping through
"That's old Sam!" Ned laughed out,
as the calf went rushing through.
The lad was shaking now with embarrassment and fright
The men were all laughing, at this ghost all brown and white
He's lost his mum, the men agreed, and of the dark is scared
So when he heard the lad, ride by, he thought it was the herd.

The lad had disappeared now, and was creeping down the road
He could not face the men again, he really felt absurd.
When next the lad came in the bar not a sound was heard
Then all at once all in the bar shouted, "have you heard?"

"Old Sam comes back to haunt us all, and give us all a fright
So be sure you're not passing Billy's yard, at the edge of night."
The lads face cracked, he broke a smile that covered all his face
The joke was good, his friends came round
and laughter filled the place.

He never passes Billy's yard, without a little smile
But he always peddles faster, along that dreaded mile.

~*~

The fifties saw the arrival in the meat industry of the co-operative farmers abattoirs, these were set up to ensure the farmer had a fair deal for his product, so instead of the farmer taking his livestock to market and hoping for a good price, the price for his product was guaranteed dependant on quality and grading system at the abattoir.

This system was first thought to be flawless, depending that the farmers for the farmers ran the abattoir, unfortunately this system was very open to CORUPTION. During the seventies this corrupt practice saw the rise and fall of a number of cooperatives.

Most abattoirs employed a manager, these were usually people who either had a farming background or a meat industry background, this would ensure that everything that was produced through the system was honestly weighed and top price paid for the product. Unfortunately the ones who were put in charge, (not all) would very soon discover how to make a bit on the side. Consequently this corruption filtered down through the ranks and everyone was involved in one sort of fiddle or another.

The first in line were the Meat and Livestock Commission, then came the managers and salesmen, then the porters, (who would load the lorries for delivery to markets) then the drivers who were at the end of the queue but took a cut for themselves, putting the losses down to bad counts on the lorries or at the farm gate.

Local deliveries to butchers shops were mostly cash transactions and deals were negotiated over the phone prior to delivery, extras were regularly sold, offal being the easiest cash product. Butchers would pay good money for a bag of liver weighing thirty pounds or more, but more often than not there would be an extra lamb or sirloin of beef.

The way it started was very simple.

After slaughtering, carcasses would be weighed and graded as to the fat content and quality, this would be undertaken whilst the carcass was still hot and wet, so weight loss due to cooling and drying out had to be assessed. This was done by the MLC under the watchful eye of an abattoir employee. He would record what the MLC quoted also the grade of the carcass. A ticket with the weight and grade was attached to the carcass, these figures would be the figures the farmer would be paid on, if the grade was good and the weight properly assessed the farmer would get a fair price for his product, sounds good.

That only applied if the farmer was at the point of weighing at the time his product came up the line and could see first hand what his product was like. Unfortunately most farmers could not undertake this due to distance or work.

The line was the never ending rail of hooks from which the carcasses were hung that came from the slaughtering area to the weighing area, from the weighing area the line went to drying or chilling points, this was where the carcasses were chosen and reweighed for loading on to trucks for delivery to customers. All sounds good?

This is how it really worked.

The line delivered the product to the weighing area, it would be weighed, several pounds were deducted for drying, the loss was calculated on how hot or wet the product was, more was taken off than was the actual loss, the carcass was graded according to the confirmation of the product, confirmation being how fat or lean the carcass was. If the product was too fat it was given a lower grade, thus getting a lesser price, there was always more fat, so the weight and grade was on the side of the abattoir. From this point the salesmen took over, they had to select the best for the customers.

The product would be re-graded, fresh tickets attached with weights and grades altered. This would give the wholesaler a lesser, or better product, depending how much kickback would be forthcoming, weight could be gained as each carcass was re-weighed individually and re-graded then the product was dispatched to meat markets, such as the Smithfield in London, Stanley meat market Liverpool or Central market Birmingham. It was very rare for the carcasses to be individually weighed, when it got to its destination, this process would take far too long, so the weight and grade would be accepted. Sometimes the wholesaler would try to fiddle the weights and attempt to get billed for less than was booked, this too led to backhanders. The better grades were given to the retailer who sent cash back with the drivers in settlement for goods received. This cash was dispersed by the abattoir and duly shared amongst whoever was involved at that level.

Whole carcasses would disappear, usually at the point of slaughter, thus no record of them was recorded by the MLC and the carcasses would then be cut up and distributed, amongst the workers and MLC.

Farmer never got paid for these, this was put down to bad counting on the farmers side, at the point of loading, quite often resulting in very heated arguments but no reimbursement was made and the farmer took a loss, this happened on a daily basis.

The farmer however would be paid on the figures the MLC would submit and had very little redress on how his product was assessed. So if the product was graded as good at the scales, the farmer would be paid on the MLC figures, little realising that his product would be reweighed and grades altered before sale.

This was common practise, no wonder the livestock industry was in such a terrible decline and meat prices soared and farmers went bankrupt, it was wholesale theft on a grand scale, the only ones who suffered were the farmer producers and the housewife.

A BIT FOR ME AND YOU

We had a little fiddle at our place of work
A bit for me, a bit for you, no one will get hurt
Just adjust the scales a bit that's all you have to do
And this will get a better price and a cut for you

Nobody will suffer, no losses it will show
The farmer he will lose a bit but that he can afford
And if he doesn't like it, he can send his goods to France
Try and get a better price he will have no chance

Every one was at it accepted by the bosses
But when the shop went bankrupt no one took the losses
Every one was out of work no jobs were left at all
Nothing in the building except the empty hall

If only things were honest and fiddles taken out
All would have employment and nobody locked out
Work would carry on with fair prices paid
And all would get a fair share each and every day.

Life was getting back to normal I was back working in the meat industry, Wendy was working as a trainee accountant and my family had almost stopped its nonsense. Then just as things were getting back to normal, something pulled the plug on us again. This was 1975.

I suffered a kind of heart attack and was forced to give up the heavy lifting job at the abattoir. The illness was caused by a virus, which settled on the pericardium sack surrounding my heart, this caused my heart to struggle and also caused severe pain, which I suffered for a week or more, thinking it was indigestion. Again if it wasn't for Wendy, I don't know what would have happened.

I remember coming home from work, at about ten at night, I was suffering very badly that night and had found it difficult to finish my shift. I came home and went straight to bed, the next thing I can remember I was on my way to the intensive care unit of Hereford hospital, being poked and tested and having wires attached to various parts of my chest. I must say that the treatment and care I received was second to none and I will never be able to thank those who looked after me enough. I had a real fright.

After a few days I decided to sign myself out as I have a morbid fear, not of hospitals so much, but of crowded places, so I felt I would be better off at home, reluctantly the hospital let me go providing I went to our local hospital in Llandrindod. On the way I made Wendy stop at Brynonnen on the pretext of taking a shower before I went to hospital, I got into bed at Brynonnen and stayed there.

I was off work for three months and when I finally went back to work, I was as weak as a kitten. So guess what? I went back to work for my old boss, back in the butchers shop. At this time he also owned a fruit and veg business a few shops away from the butchers. He would hide at the fruit shop, it had a back room he converted into an office from where he controlled his empire and kept out of sight of those who wanted money.

TWIT

I really was a silly twit
To go and work for a nit like this
To suffer abuse at every turn
For goodness sake will I never learn?

A plan now hatched inside my head
To buy him out was my intent
Greengrocer's shop he also owned
Sell it to me I was so bold

To this he readily agreed
And to the bank on my fastest steed
The manager readily agreed
And made the deal with the greatest speed

My own boss I was at last
And thought here I am at last
A shopkeeper I am here to stay
I think I'll join the Chamber of Trade

Wendy and I had at last put the gossips to rest and were accepted as a married couple, we loved Brynonnen and Penybont and got to know a lot of very nice people there, but wherever you find people there is scandal and a very interesting scandal was unfolding.

Chapter Eight

Habits of a lifetime are very hard to break, so when you do the same thing every morning for twenty years it's very difficult to get out of the routine you have unconsciously set yourself.

John was such a creature of habit, each morning he would rise at the same hour, he would stumble to the kitchen, put the kettle on, shoo the cat off the cooker hood where it would have slept, warmed by the pilot light, then as the kettle was boiling, shave and dress.

He would open the bathroom window, check the weather; this window afforded him a view of the hills. On his return to the kitchen he'd make the tea, take a cup for his wife, Sally, who would remain in bed not wanting to get in the way, as she could be a little irritable first thing and rather than risk cross words, found this the safer option.

They lived almost separate lives. They were very fond of each other and family always came first, as far as a social or sexual side to the relationship, they were none existent. In fact, they had grown more like brother and sister than husband and wife, they would stand firmly together for each other or their daughters and always in their own way put on a great show of affection when in company. They tolerated each other's indiscretions, almost to the point of ignoring they existed.

John liked to think of himself as the local squire, a position he had created for himself, after tireless years serving the community on the local town council as Mayor and representative for the town in many guises. Tourism was his favourite, he travelled all over the country, all expenses paid, in the hope of selling the delights of the town, which were few.

He had two main passions, he was very involved in harness racing, and horses came very high on his list of importance, both in the breeding and racing, although the latter had been left to lapse because of time spent serving the town council.

His other passion was a woman friend called Sue. Sue ran a small but very profitable riding school and had just taken delivery of a new Range Rover to pull her horsebox. She was married to a very successful solicitor whose practice, established by his father, was the biggest in town, respected by all. The practice employed some twenty people, and the Clerk of the Court had his office in the same chambers. This almost guaranteed a throughput of potential customers for the practise, as any court business done out of hours was conducted there.

There were two brothers in the practise, one was unmarried, he was the youngest and the most approachable. Although he was ruthless in court, he led a very private life. He spent most of his free time in his house by the local boating lake. In addition he valued his privacy and did not socialise in the town. Sue's husband on the other hand, although a mild spoken man, was prone to violent outbursts. He was not a violent man physically but could cut you to pieces with his tongue. Both John and Sue lived in close proximity to each other, the only thing separating them was a shared piece of pastureland, jointly owned, there was a covenant on it forbidding any building, so in order to utilise it they had jointly purchased it.

John, after having a cup of tea would go out into the yard to start his morning tasks.

The house was a grand house, far too big for him and his wife but it was a status symbol. It was reached by a driveway through a set of very smart wooden gates, these had been commissioned from a local carpenter who owed him a favour. They were never paid for but the carpenter did get a council house, town councillors got many favours.

The drive grew into a large courtyard, an open fronted garage to one side with room for two cars, but it only housed a 1901 governess cart, which was John's pride and joy, and Ben. Ben was the Border collie; he lived in a kennel built into the side of the garage. The drive led up to a stable block where three horses were stabled.

Across the road from the house was a large paddock where the horses were put each morning. First thing John did was call Ben and feed him. Then he would take out his favourite pipe, stuff a pinch of tobacco into the bowl, then taking out a box of matches strike one and light the pipe, cupping his hands around the bowl to protect the flame, blow out the match and put the spent match in his trouser pocket. This he did out of habit, as he once discarded a match carelessly and started a fire. He then made his way to the stables, smoke swirling around his head as he walked, closely followed by Ben sniffing as he went and cocking his leg up at a fence post. It was the same fence post every morning, Ben too was a creature of habit.

The horses waited, for him to let them into the paddock. He would fuss over each horse in turn and feed each a polo mint, asking; 'which of you will take me around the lake this morning?'

The town John loved so much nestled in a valley surrounded by rolling hills. On one side was the golf course, a very important meeting place for all the well-to-do, and, if you were lucky, the not-so-well-to-do, it was a case of who you knew rather than the size of your bank balance that got you into the golf click. It is a good golf course well maintained and well used, it overlooks the town and the views are spectacular.

The town, Victorian in its architecture, has buildings that are big and red bricked. Some have reverted to apartments, some are slums, the slums grew from utter neglect during the 1960s, when a family of property investors moved to the town and bought all the large buildings. They let them out to the Department of Health and Social Security; this caused a dramatic down turn in the class structure as a number of unemployed moved to the town with the promise of fresh air and a new start. The main shopping area consists of only one street of any consequence. The council in their wisdom decided to let a supermarket chain move in.

John had fought against this but was defeated, this almost wiped out the small trader, most of the food shops closed within the first six months. The town council having as much forward vision as it is possible to get whilst looking in a mirror. So it came as no surprise that the town slipped into a decline it would never crawl out of.

However, John was a big fish in a small pond and felt the town would soon recover and prosper, so he called on every one to change trades if need be and try to weather out the storm. Most did change, a butchers became a trinket shop, a fishmonger became a delicatessen and a number of building societies moved in. Therefore, overall, the town took on a different look, the supermarket prospered and those who did change did a reasonable trade, those who did not change closed.

John chose the horse to hitch to the governess cart, he then led the others to the paddock and watched as they galloped and kicked their way around the field, running off the restrictions they had been under all night.

Relighting his pipe and putting the spent match in his pocket he walked back to the stable exchanging a morning greeting with a neighbour who was exercising his dog. He then fed the remaining horse a few handfuls of oats before harnessing it to the cart for the morning trot around the lake.

He put on a brown work coat and adjusted his hat, he always wore a hat, he had many and varied hats. After filling and relighting his pipe, putting the match in his pocket, he climbed into the cart and said, “walk on”, the horse started forward slowly at first, then picked up pace when it had settled into the rhythm. All the while swirls of smoke from John’s pipe drifted behind the pair as they made for the lake.

The lake situated on a plateau, and was reached by going through a wooded area of private land. John had long had permission to use this route, the only other way to the lake was by way of a very steep hill and this was too much of a pull for John’s horses so the easier route was taken.

Further up the hill leading from the lake was the golf course, the road was busy with golfers, eager to get in a morning round, they had to travel around the lake to get to the road leading to the golf course. The speed limit was restricted to ten miles an hour so speeding vehicles were rare. There were people walking or riding bicycles around the lake, a few like John with horses, the lake being flanked on one side by a common where horses were galloped along a bridal path.

All was going well, the horse was pulling well, the morning was crisp, a slight frost had fallen the previous night making the road slightly slippery in places but with care not a danger. The lake was still and calm, the two resident swans were gliding across the lake, their reflection mirrored in the glassy water. Ducks and moorhens also lived on the lake and each year a toad patrol was set up in order to safe guard the toad population. No boats were out as it was not yet summer and all the boats were being repaired and varnished in the boathouse.

Several people were feeding bread to the ducks, they waved to John as he trotted by, not all of them liked John but it was considered a courtesy to wave, more at the horse than John.

Surrounding the lake on the other side was woodland and as John was enjoying the morning, a car, exceeding the speed limit, sped past. The horse took fright and John fought to control the animal as it reared up in the shafts. John was concerned the horse would damage itself and the cart and struggled to get it under control. He managed to calm the horse down then he stepped from the cart to go to the front of the horse, to give it a reassuring stroke when another car sped past and frightened the animal again.

John at this time was very vulnerable, he had the reigns in his hand, the horse lurched forward, John lost his footing and fell, the wheel of the cart went over his lower leg. John felt it break, he still held on to the reigns despite being in agonising pain determined he was not going to lose the horse.

The pain John suffered was unbearable; he was on the point of fainting when a group of people came to his aid. The horse and cart were taken into the wooded area in an attempt to calm the horse down. An ambulance was sent for, someone had put a coat over John to keep him warm as he was suffering from shock. A woman retrieved John's hat and pipe; John had bitten through the stem of his pipe during the incident and had swallowed the part of the stem he had bitten off.

He was transported to hospital, it was not a big hospital but well run. It had a well-fitted theatre and a resident surgeon who was an old friend of John's. On his arrival he was treated like a V.I.P. He was taken to x-ray and apart from a broken lower leg, a few bruises and a swallowed pipe stem, which he was assured would pass, maybe a little painfully, he was lucky he had not suffered more.

His leg was set, a full leg plaster being applied, this was to keep him still, which was felt a necessary precaution. John was installed in a side ward and Sally was informed. The horse and cart had been returned to the house and un-harnessed, the horse put into the field with the others, the cart, slightly damaged, put into the garage.

Sally visited John and was relieved he was not badly hurt, also silently gloating; he would not be chasing Sue in the near future. She made sure he was comfortable and assured him after a night in hospital he would be home next day. Then bidding him farewell with a reluctant peck on the cheek, more for show than affection, ordering him to rest and not cause a fuss, she went about her business.

Sally worked for a tour company, as tour coaches arrived in the town she would arrange trips around the surrounding countryside. She had done this for a number of years and had made many friends, both in Britain and on the continent.

Sue turned up to see what damage her lover had sustained. After the initial shock, seeing John, plastered up to the thigh, her concern was for the forthcoming first Meet of the hunt. This was due to take place in a month and by the extent of the break to John's leg, he would not be taking up the Hunt Master's position for the first Meet and maybe not the season. John tried to allay her worries, saying he was a fast healer and the plaster would be off and he would be Master for the first Meet. Sue stayed for a while, stroking John's forehead until he fell asleep, then gently kissed his forehead and left.

Over the next few weeks, Sally had the task of feeding Ben and letting the horses into the paddock. She knew that John and Sue were involved, but each morning when she saw Sue she waved politely, while all the time smiling between gritted teeth. She would have her revenge one day and the thought of that kept her going.

All the while John was incapacitated, Sally played little tricks on him, not hurtful, but just enough to let him know she was the one who was looking after him. She would make him cups of tea and leave them just out of reach, she would help him to the bathroom, and then go out for half an hour, letting him sit there, shouting for help. She'd go out at night leaving him alone, putting on just enough perfume to leave him wondering who she was meeting, forgetting to cook his evening meal, making the excuse that she was not used to him being home in the evenings. Sally took great delight in winding John up, knowing he could not retaliate.

Sue would wait for Sally to leave the house, walk up the paddock, making sure she was not seen, and sit with John, the break was not healing as fast as it should, her concerns were becoming a reality. The pipe stem had passed and with a little more pain than expected, but a few whiskies and a soft cushion sorted it out.

It was time to make alternative arrangements. It was evident John would not be able to ride. Sue said she would not be riding either. Instead, she would transport John in the Range Rover, so he could at least watch some of the Meet.

A trial run was organised, Sue drove the Range Rover to John's house and with the aid of crutches, John managed to sit on the seat, but due to the length of plaster, his leg would not fit into the car. So another plan was hatched, they phoned the hospital and asked them to cut the plaster just below the knee so his leg would fit. The doctor was sent for, the situation explained and the solution arrived at. John would attend the outpatients in a few days; the leg would be x-rayed and providing the results were favourable, the plaster cut. The results were good; the plaster was cut with strict instructions not to attempt to ride a horse.

John felt a freedom from the weight of the cast and was able to walk unaided, he had almost forgotten what it was like to be somewhere near independent and it felt good.

Sue had planned a surprise. On the day of the hunt she would organise a picnic basket, roast chicken, salad, eggs, cheese, wine and coffee, plus fruit salad for afters. The day would be special, after all, if John could not take his place as Master, she was going to make sure the day was marked in some other way. If the weather were fine, she would set the picnic at some vantage point, where they could watch some of the Hunt; if the weather turned wet, the picnic would take place in the Range Rover.

Sally was not pleased with the arrangement; she felt that it was not appropriate that they should be so public, if the affair was going to become common knowledge then at least have the courtesy to file for divorce first. John said that there was no affair, the friendship was purely platonic and the arrangements were going ahead.

Sally had made her point and was determined if this arrangement was going to take place despite her feelings then she would have to take action herself. Sally knew that Sue would drop him like a hot brick if divorce was mentioned, and as Sue's husband was a very well respected solicitor, the chance of divorce were very slim indeed, Sue would not throw away all the fringe benefits her position bought her.

John improved daily, the bruising had all but disappeared, he had no pain from his leg, he had managed a trip to the local hotel, where the Hunt Meet was going to take place in order to finalise arrangements. He did try to saddle and mount his hunter, but the effort was a little too much, so he decided to accept the offer of a day in the Range Rover, despite Sally's disapproval.

The night before the hunt, John was getting a real ear-bashing from Sally. He tried to lie his way out of the affair but she knew he was lying. They slept in separate rooms. This was serious, although their relationship was not as it should be they never slept apart. Sally locked him out.

John rose at the usual hour and set about his routine, he did not take tea to Sally, not because of his plastered leg, he had long been able to manage stairs, but for fear she would do something silly. He had visions of her locking him in the bathroom all day, so he kept out of her way. He dressed, had tea, fed the dog; let the horses out, but still no sign of Sally. Her car was still in the drive, so she must be sulking, John dismissed the problem.

At nine am Sue arrived with the Range Rover, picnic basket and blankets to keep off the chill if they sat outside. John shouted up the stairs to Sally to say he was leaving, no reply came and he had it in his mind to go up but felt it would probably be the wrong thing to do.

They set off, full of anticipation of a good days hunting, and whatever else, came their way. The first stop was at the largest hotel in the town. It was a tradition, the hunt, booted and spurred, would meet and take the stirrup cup. John would not miss this tradition, not when he was supposed to be the Master, he wanted to wish all a good day.

After partaking of the stirrup cup and a word with the temporary Hunt Master and whipper in, John and Sue set off to a location, suggested by the Master.

The day was fine, a clear blue sky and a light breeze. A good day for hunting, Sue and John were going to have a wonderful day. They had a warm car, a picnic and they were looking forward to a good day. Then, in the evening, dinner back at the hotel.

Unknown to John, Sally had put another plan into action. She'd arranged for herself and a friend to have an extended tour of Europe starting in Amsterdam. She emptied the freezer, nothing edible was left in the house, poured his stock of whisky down the sink and had cut the plugs off everything electrical, leaving only six inches of cable. He was oblivious to all that was before him.

Sally was on the warpath, and hell hath no fury like a Sally scorned.

The day for John was going well, they had found a corner of a field to park, it was a little cold so they decided to remain in the car, for the time being anyway. They looked across the fields towards a wooded area; this is where the Master had told them they would be heading, they settled down to wait.

John and Sue were two normally sensible adults but passion is a strange phenomenon, when it takes over nothing can stop the rush of blood and the tide of passion. No words were spoken, the picnic basket was put out, the seats folded back and the blankets unfolded, John and Sue were locked in each other, the plastered leg caused a little discomfort, but when the going gets tough…

How strange passion is, nothing gets in its way, your senses, apart from the ones that have taken over, seem to switch off. They were so involved threshing about in the back of the Range Rover, neither of them heard what was coming their way.

In the woods the hunt was on the scent, a fox had broken cover and was running across the field towards the lover's car. The whipper-in, blew his horn and off the hunt set, full gallop through the wood. The whipper-in was first to break cover and seeing the Range Rover in the corner of the field, felt very pleased with himself for giving the invalided Master a great view. Little did he know what was going on, until it was too late!

The fox, in full flight was heading straight for the car followed by the hounds and the whipper-in. The main hunt followed close behind. The fox darted under the car and into scrubland behind it, this was more than the whipper-in could hope for in his wildest dreams, this was surly going to score points with the new Master, bringing the hunt directly to him, what a great day this was turning out to be. The whipper-in came close to the car, hoping to catch sight of the couple, his intention was to doff his cap politely and set off again in pursuit of raynard. What he did see astounded him, the lovers, threshing about under the blanket oblivious to all.

The hunt was approaching very quickly. His only way of warning of the ensuing drama was to blow his horn. This he did, he blew as he had never blown before, so much so that John jumped up so quickly, he hit the roof of the car with such force as to cause a dent in it. Then there was the sheer panic, with both trying to steal the blanket off each other in order to cover their embarrassment.

The hunt had arrived, it was no use the whipper-in trying to steer them away, all were watching the commotion, some of the older women were trying to shield the youngsters from seeing such debauchery, but with not much success.

After what seemed like hours, the temporary Master managed to muster the hunt into some sort of semblance, and move on, all the time sniggering to himself, he knew that he was going to see the season out, the Master would not dare show his face again. The hunt moved away, after filing past the car all doffing caps as they went.

John and Sue sat for a long time not saying a word to each other, they sorted themselves out and decided the best thing was to go home and wait for whatever came.

The picnic basket was never retrieved. Not many words were spoken on the never ending drive home. Sue dropped John at his gate, rather than risk going into the yard where Sally could be waiting, 12 bore shotgun in hand.

John was shaking as he opened the door. He called out to Sally, not very loudly, there was no reply. He felt slight relief at this, at least he could have whisky for courage. He went into the living room to get a glass of his amber tipple, it was gone, he went into the kitchen. In the sink were four empty whisky bottles, what had she done, this was sacrilege. The gun cabinets, he always kept a bottle there, it was empty. He hobbled from room to room wondering what was going on? He decided on a cup of coffee, there was none, no coffee, tea, milk, sugar, the fridge and freezer were empty. This was serious. He saw a letter on the table and tore at the envelope.

Dear John, I have left for a trip around Europe - you are paying. Do not look for food there is none, maybe Sue will feed you. I don't know if or when I will return, but thanks for the holiday.

Sally. PS: Don't forget to feed Ben.

What did she mean you are paying for it? John broke into a cold sweat, what had she done, he was just about to phone a taxi to take him to town for some food when the phone rang. He almost jumped out of his skin, he picked up the receiver, expecting it to be Sally, a voice spoke, a very calm voice.

"Hello John how are you?"

"I'm fine," said John, "who's speaking?"

No name was given, just a chilling message, keep away from my wife or you may have two broken legs. John's blood ran cold; he replaced the receiver and stood looking at it for what seemed hours. The game was up, they were discovered, what repercussions were going to follow? What was he going to do now? Sally had left, he was on his own. Taxi, yes that is the answer, go to town and find out if the news had been broadcast. He need not have bothered, the hunt had returned and were at the hotel for dinner. The topic of conversation was the Range Rover.

The taxi arrived and John stepped in. First, he went to a friend who knew of the affair. John told all over a sandwich and a glass of whisky.

"What should I do?" Asked John.

"Well," said his friend, "I would lie low for a few days, but in the morning, I would check your bank and find out how you are paying for Sally's trip."

Meanwhile at the hotel the hunt dinner was in full swing, the conversation was still on the discovery of John and Sue in the Range Rover. The whipper-in was being bought drinks just to hear the tale repeated, each time it was told something new was added. He was going to dine out on this for many a long day.

The mood however was a little more sombre at Sue's house. Her husband was laying down the law, who better than him to do it considering his position in the town. The Range Rover was to be sold, as he did not need the reminder of this affair staring him in the face as he went out each morning, Sue was to quit the Hunt and never be alone with John again. All conditions were agreed, she knew which side she needed to stay on and put up no arguments. She knew she would have to work very hard at putting her marriage back together and was prepared to do anything to wipe out the events of that day. Overall, she considered she had been let off very lightly indeed.

John did not sleep easy that night, he tossed and turned, and woke up after a nightmarish dream involving him and Sue being chased naked through a wood by a pack of hounds, it was so real John was soaked with perspiration and shaking.

The day dawned misty, John rose and went into his routine, all he managed was to feed Ben and put the horses out, there was no tea, even his tobacco supply had disappeared, and he was distraught. He phoned the bank, the account was seriously depleted and several thousand pounds had been withdrawn. John was incensed, he began shouting at the cat. He took out his pipe and stuffing the last of his tobacco into the bowl and sucked violently as he put the match to it, thinking as he was lighting up should he discard this match? Set the lot ablaze, she would have nothing to come back to. He had second thoughts, as he realised he would be homeless as well. He settled down, took a few puffs of his pipe and decided to ring the doctor and ask when the plaster could come off his leg, at least he would be more mobile when it was removed.

The doctor said it could be removed in about a week; this at least was good news. After a few moments, he had gathered his thoughts, he could see this disruption through, after all, worse things happen at sea.

He telephoned for supplies; the local shop would still deliver so he put in an order, top of the list, whisky and tobacco. Next to ring was an electrician to put new leads and plugs on all the appliances, at least he would have food, drink and television.

A few days passed with no visitors then one evening just as he was settling down the doorbell rang.

At the door was a representation from the local council. Three of them stood at the door looking very sheepish. Trying not to make eye contact with John, he asked them in, he offered each in turn a drink, they declined.

"Well it's nice to have visitors," said John.

The visitors looked at each other, then the one who had been selected as spokesman stood up.

"It's like this John," he said, "It's about the other day, the council feel that you should resign, for the town's sake."

John was stunned, he sat back in his chair and looked blank, after all the year's service he had shown to the community this was the thanks he got.

"Who's bright idea was this?" John retorted, "one bloody mistake and you want me to resign?"

The spokesman answered. "It's all over town John and this request is not just from the council it comes from the private sector, in fact John, it has been formally requested by a law firm."

John knew his days were numbered.

"They feel that if you remain on the council, any decision the council may make in the future could be compromised."

John's heart sunk, he had no alternative, he resigned.

Sally returned a month later, she found John cleaning out the stables, she did not make a big effort to explain her actions, only to say he'd had his fling and let's hear no more about it. She listened sympathetically to his tale over the council and offered no comment.

Moreover, true to her word, she never spoke of the incident again. John for his part started work for the tourism board for Wales and continued to sell the town, all over Europe accompanied by Sally.

THE DENT

Cars were on the forecourt, shining clean and bright
There must have been a hundred, glistening in the light
Small ones at the front were placed, for searching eyes to catch
And as the rows went away, the biggest at the back

I looked across the rows of cars, all neatly in a line
But couldn't make my mind up, I was taking time
When all at once as if by magic, a salesman did appear
All one owner, best of care, low mileage, he did sneer

We went into the garage, a Range Rover I did spy
On the roof a great big bulge, was reaching for the sky
It's quite a funny story, of how this bump appeared
It happened at the local hunt, at the turning of the year

The lady who did own it, and on who the blame must rest
Had a fancy for the master, whose hunt was always best
But the master took a tumble, and landed with a wallow
So the Range Rover it was offered, for the hunt to follow

The lady who was driving, and the master of the hunt
Got in front of all the hounds, and hid behind a hump
They did not hear the hounds go by, baying in the wind
So when the whipper-in came by, his eyes were put to dim

To warn them was his only thought, as to his lips to blast
His hunting horn he blew aloud, as he went riding past
The master who was busy, and hearing the blast so clear
Nearly jumped out of his skin, as he leaped up in the air

His head it hit the roof, you see with terrible resound
And as they grappled for their clothes, the hunt did gather round
On seeing what was going on, they gave a mighty cheer
But the master's head was aching, and he wished he wasn't here

The lady sold the car you see, to save embarrassment
As everyone who looked at it, knew about the dent
The master and the lady, don't speak much any more
And the whipper-in, who tells the tale, is always asked for more.

Out on our own

I was fed up with being taken advantage of, my boss would hide away all day in the fruit and veg shop leaving me to run the butchers shop. I felt I needed more of a challenge in my life so I offered to buy him out and take over the butchers shop. He did not agree to this as the butchers was not really his to sell, it was still part of the family empire, although he would sell me the fruit and veg shop. So Wendy and I went to the bank arranged a loan and with Brynonnen as collateral we bought the fruit and veg shop. We had arrived.

I knew nothing about fruit or veg, but within a month, I knew as much as anybody and I really enjoyed it. It was a good trade to be in, no blood or flies, profits were good and business grew at an alarming rate. We refitted the shop and were employing one full time girl and two part time school kids to help stock the shelves at night, and had help through the day from a friend who had a box of groceries at the end of the week in payment. We were so proud of ourselves, but pride comes before a fall, little did we know in ten years we would be fighting for our very existence.

We were invited to join the Chamber of Trade. What a joke, Chamber of Trade, they might just as well have been called chamber pot, they worked hand in glove with the local council and had as much foresight as a mole. Anything constructive that was suggested was usually put to the back of the agenda or thrown out, between these two bodies, which should have been corpses they succeeded in running the town into the ground. Investment was none existent. One of the events organised was late night shopping at Christmas.

It was decided that at Christmas time all those shops who

were in the main street would contribute to a free hot soup stand, to try and encourage shoppers out later in the evening. Each trader chipped in a few pounds and a stand was set up, it had little success, except with the afternoon drinkers who were making their way home from the pub and decided to stop off for a freebee. What a farce. The only person to benefit from this wondrous event was the local ironmonger.

THE HARDWARE MAN

The traders held a meeting, first Tuesday of the month
And at these monthly meetings, grumbles they would hump
The chairman was of little use and sat as if were dead
So everyone would scream and shout and just go off their head.

The meetings they were terrible, no problems they would solve
The only thing agreed upon was who should be involved
It was decided soup be served to shoppers in the street
At Christmas time so everyone should have a little treat.

We all agreed to make it free, donations were collected
On how to heat up all this soup, this task it was neglected
Then all at once the hardware man, offered his assistance
An old gas stove was fitted up, now we were in business.

This treat it was to last, for three days of the week
And we were told upon the stove, our eyes we were to keep
We guarded it all the time and safe we did it keep
Until the dustman came around, at the ending of the week.

A stove he spied, just left alone by the back door of a shop
And as his own stove had just blown up he thought 'oh well why not'.
If ever we asked this man, a gas stove for to move
He'd look at us with blanked out eyes and walk away quite rude.

So when the ironmonger heard about this plight
His charity gave out on him and moaned all day and night.
The Chamber had to meet his bill, it was one hundred pounds
For an old gas cooker he has paid just a mere five pounds.

This hardware man is still around, he's only four feet tall
So when he steps off pavements, it's like falling off a wall
So when one day while walking out, I spied him in the gutter
I laughed so much, I nearly cried as he fumbled and he stuttered.

The best place he had found at last, for his turned up nose
This most charitable of gentleman, who charges for a stove.
The five pounds that he paid for it, was so cheap a price
To guarantee the friendship of all that met his price.

The Chairperson, or President as they liked to be called, tried to control everything that was planned. There was no delegation so there was always great confusion, consequently all the eggs were put in one basket and most were broken. No matter what was attempted throughout the year, whatever the Chamber of Trade touched failed to materialise, or if it did succeed, it was surrounded by chaos and panic. We left the Chamber of Trade, thanking our lucky stars we had not got more involved.

We were offered bigger premises, we took it and expanded the business, we now sold fruit and veg, fresh meat and delicatessen, cheese, bread, poultry, fresh fish and a myriad of spices and things in tins I never had the courage to try. This was good, trade was good and we were getting good at being shopkeepers.

Eight years down the line and only one holiday, we were offered a trip to Denmark by the Danish Bacon Company at a reduced rate. So with several other traders and a temporary passport, off we went for a long weekend to Esbjerg, to visit their factory and have a few days on the high seas. This was my first trip to foreign parts and the trip was very informative, we saw how the other half lived and came home with renewed ambition and a notebook full of ideas. But disaster was coming at us at a hundred miles an hour, thanks to the council planning and probably a few well placed brown envelopes full of money. This happened all over the country but nobody expected it to happen in Llandrindod Wells. A supermarket was going to be built right behind us in Tudor Lane.

When this supermarket opened it caused us a great deal of trade loss. Not just for us but a lot of small shops suffered at the hands of this retail giant who had no regard for the small business man, bringing this retail disaster into our small town led to the ultimate demise of the town. As trade fell off at an alarming rate, we could not compete with the prices offered by the new unwelcome competitor, we sought the help of the bank. The bank had appointed a new manager who, along with the new supermarket, managed to put a few shops out of business. The bank manager's name was, Geoffrey Hardy.

We had to engage the services of a new accountant, the greatly feared John Duggan Esq., from Hay-on-Wye. John was a very round jolly man who certainly knew his job. He also liked his horses and snooker along with a lust for fine wines and good food of which he indulged greatly, hence his roundness. We called on him for assistance, as this new bank manager was giving us a very hard time. John Duggan was a very clever man and with his help we put Mr Hardy to flight. I have heard that this particular bank manager was moved sideways, so to speak, to stop him putting more people out of business.

It's true what people say about banks, they will lend you an umbrella when the sun shines but at the first drop of rain they want the umbrella back. I have heard so many stories of farms being put out of business and farmers committing suicide because of pressure bought to bear by banks tightening the screws. I can honestly say that had we not got out when we did I don't dare to think what may have become of us. The bank was called the Midland Bank but has since changed to H.S.B.C.

MIDLAND MAN

When first our future we did plan
Against all odds we did span
To get a business was the plan
So we went to meet the Midland man.

He sat behind his desk so grand
And offered us a helping hand
We talked a lot and made our stand
And shook hands with this Midland man.

The business well it did expand
And we invested several grand
And everyone asked ‘who is this man?’
We told them he’s the Midland man.

One morning at my door did stand
A stranger who held out his hand
‘Pardon,’ I said ‘I don’t understand’.
He had arrived; the new Midland man

At this my spirits did expand
A new man to lend a helping hand
How wrong I was to understand
The motives of the Midland man.

Consolidate was his command
No money left to help expand
The bank you see has made a stand
Said this squeaky little Midland man.

We had to summon up a plan
With best friends we cooked a plan
We’d call in our accountant man
To cool this red hot Midland man.

J. Duggan came and made his stand
And he did wonders with this man
In knots so tight he strung this ham
Who called himself the Midland man.

We changed our business, the supermarket had taken most of our trade, so we turned into a sandwich bar and coffee shop selling some delicatessen products as a side line. We served breakfasts, lunches and afternoon teas, then during the Victorian week we served Champaign and smoked salmon. For a while it looked as if the change was going to work but it did not make enough to keep us there.

We had to sell, we came out of the business with about three thousand pounds, after everything was paid and, with nowhere to live, we had to get out of town we did not feel that we could have survived there any longer so decisions were made. It's a strange feeling leaving the home you had worked so hard for, with nothing but what we could carry in a trailer behind the car. Not knowing what the future held, our only option was to move south.

We moved our lives. I was leaving my hometown for the second time in my life and vowed never to return. It seemed to me the harder I tried to get on, the more I got pushed down, we had to uproot Kirk, this move caused him more distress than he ever let on and I felt very bitter towards everyone in that one horse town. Leaving Landrindod we left behind some very fond memories and a few very special friends, some great characters, one such was locally known as Pip.

Pip was a local builder and gravedigger, the latter job being done with great reverence, although sometimes slightly under the influence of some libation or other, to keep out the cold.

Pip was strolling through the local park one evening when he came upon a pheasant struggling to get free from a bramble bush, which by the way was laden with blackberries, and as everyone knows, pheasant and blackberry sauce is very nice indeed, but this was the last thing on Pip's mind.

He managed to release the stricken bird at great cost to his skin, which was badly scratched by the brambles, only to discover the bird had a broken wing, so he took it to the vet. The advise given by the vet was best to wring its neck as he did not think the bird would be any use except for the pot. Well this was not what Pip wanted so at great cost the bird was patched up and taken home to recover. Pip's wife was none too keen to have the bird in the house, so a temporary run was made in the garden and after a month or two the bird got well, due to Pip's feeding and care. The vet's diagnosis was full recovery and release back into the wild was recommended, so it was to be.

This was hard for Pip as he had grown quite fond of the bird, but his wife had given the ultimatum; 'that bird goes, or I do!' So it had to go. Pip found a box and put the pheasant into it, then set off towards the park, where he had found it, he set the box down on the ground behind a large hedge, thinking the bird would seek cover but to his surprise, when the box was opened, the bird flew straight up into the air.

What Pip or the pheasant did not know, behind the hedge was a local farmer named Billy Evans who was out shooting, and as soon as he saw the bird flying into the air 'end of pheasant'. Pip was incensed, he went mad and threatened to shoot Billy who by now was running away as fast as he could. Pip gathered up the pheasant, took it home and he buried it in the garden. It is said he cried over it for some time, how sad.

Some people are so soft hearted, it makes you wonder how they cope with the world as it is today, full of hunger and violence, maybe they just ignore it, in the hope it will pass them by.

PIP

A gentle giant of a man, who never hurt a fly
He spent his days in innocence with a welcome pint
A builder and a gravedigger, were his income source
And walking round the parkland, he'd stop and take a pause
He never caused disturbance or got in any fight
He'd stagger home from the pub almost every night

Ask him for a helping hand, he was first in line
Never once was Pip late, he was always there on time
His kindness to the animals and children just the same
Everybody missed Pip, when he got to the end of the game.

I had given up my shooting at this time and when I think I could have been on the other side of the hedge I count my blessing I was not, I gave up shooting because of a pheasant and its colours.

A LOVELY SHADE OF GREEN

While walking with my dog one day, gun under my arm
Along a wooded footpath a pheasant he did run
My dog started after it, but stopped with such a fluffer
Sun shining through the wood, it caught the pheasant's colour

The gold and greens were vibrant, in that morning sun
As I loaded up a cartridge in the barrel of my gun
When I took my aim at him, I stopped to take the scene
Of colours gold and brown and a lovely shade of green.

I lowered my gun to view it all, my dog, she sat as well
The colours of that pheasant, held us in his spell
And as I looked I lowered my gun, to view the entire scene
Of colours gold and brown and a lovely shade of green.

I put the gun away that day and never shot again
The old dog lived to retirement, never to hunt again
I never missed the shooting, or the hunting scene
But I won't forget the colours, of gold and brown and green.

Another tale of Pip, one day when he was at the grave digging, as I said he did like a wee drink, so when he had this particular job to do he was in a state, not falling about, but happy. He was busily digging away, when he felt very sleepy, so he sat in the bottom of the grave to have a smoke and a rest. As he was resting a lady, who was visiting her husband's grave a short distance away, was frightened by him emerging out of the ground, stretching and moaning. She took to her heels and ran out of the cemetery, very distressed, it took a long time to assure her that it was not someone coming back to haunt her. She finally did see the funny side of it but she called out each time she visited the cemetery, just to see if anyone was there.

Reg

This tale concerns a guy called Reg.

Reg was a motorcycle fanatic, he was brilliant with bikes and he could build anything to your design, and often marry two or three different bikes and re-name it a special.

Reg had an accident, which left him partially disabled so his motorcycle trials days were cut short, but after a few years rest he decided to have one more go. With the support of his friends, which may I add were many, he decided to enter the Welsh two day's trial.

Anyone who has ever entered this event will tell you it is gruelling, you need plenty of stamina and a lot of guts. Reg entered on a Greevs 250cc, this was a bike he had rebuilt and adapted himself and it was some sort of machine. He set off on day one of the trial, during which the riders have to check in to various points throughout the day, Reg was making good time and even managed to complete day one, a great feat, considering he had not ridden for some years.

Reg was very distinctive, he always had a half smoked liquorice paper cigarette in his mouth, this he would chew on until it eventually fell apart, then as if by magic another would appear to take its place. Another feature of Reg was he used to talk through his nose, if you didn't know him it took some while to make out what he was saying.

Day two arrived and found Reg, much the worse for wear, as stiffness had set in overnight and he had to have assistance to mount his machine, but once on board, he was off like the proverbial bullet. Stage one went by without too much trouble, but the next stage was a lunch break and this found Reg in trouble, he had to dismount. To add to his trouble he had developed cramp in his legs, so as he approached the checkpoint, he began to shout, 'help, I can't get off'. This set the marshals off, trying to run alongside Reg and gain control of his bike, some of them fell by the wayside, laughing too much to be of any assistance, and others were shouting, 'what are you trying to say?' The hilarity this debacle caused was amazing, marshals were falling into mud pools, as Reg was trying in vain to circle in order to gain help, when all of a sudden the bike stalled and both Reg and the bike fell sideways, burning his cramped leg on the exhaust. This was the last ride for Reg, but it was talked about for years and never failed to raise a laugh . I think Reg deserves local folk hero status for his services to the motorcycle.

THE HERO REG

Reg, is mounted on his steed, all the warnings he did not heed
Off into the mist he rode, fag in gob and chest so bold
On the Greevs across the rough, he used to be oh so tough
Riding like a thing possessed, passes traffic on the rough
Weaving here and dodging there, didn't seem to have a care
First day done, that's not too bad, off to bed, one last fag
Day two did dawn a stiffer Reg, hardly managed out of bed
Must put on a real brave face to give up now, a real disgrace
Gets upon his trusty steed, into the mist he did speed
Reg gets up to the lunchtime break, panic on his screwed up face
'I can't get off!' Reg did cry, 'help me for I fear I'll die!'
Marshals rushing to his aid, falling about in an awful state
Poor old Reg he fell off, sod the bike was his final quaff.

The bitterness I felt about leaving my business has gone now, but at the time I was very angry, I had a lot to offer to Llandrindod. Me, John Duggan and another interested party had been in negotiation with the then Welsh Development Agency. I had a plan for a run down garage, The Automobile Palace had all but closed down so I approached the owner with a tentative offer, which was readily accepted subject to planning regulations being granted. Overtures had been made to several leisure companies and we had received positive responses to all but one.

Everything was set to go, funded by several large organisations that John Duggan and I had been in touch with. It would have put the town right back on the map and given employment to fifty or more people, but there was the council and Licensed Victuals. They in their wisdom put a stop to it and all the plans that the W.D.A. had were scrapped, despite pleas from the W.D.A. and ourselves. Through the short sightedness of the town council and one councillor in particular, Mary Booth, who made it her business to stop us, the town lost out. I firmly believe that had we been given the go ahead on this project we would still be there now, maybe it's just as well it did not happen, or the next stage of our lives would not have made us work harder and Kirk would not have got to university, but who knows.

Wendy had suffered greatly at the hands of Llandrindod and at my stubbornness. I was going down fighting but I was too blind to see I was dragging Wendy and Kirk down with me. Wendy left me for a while, she took Kirk and went to her mothers, I managed to get her back promising to sell the shop and move south. I was terrified and very ashamed, I had failed and let down my family, what was to become of us, we had sold Brynonnen to appease the bank but it only held them at bay, until John Duggan got us out of trouble, we were almost bankrupt.

We moved in with Wendy's mother. I was dreading this, the shame and humiliation I felt were almost unbearable. We had lost everything and I was totally to blame, what chance had we to start again, as far as I was concerned we had no chance. She was very good about it, but we felt terrible, she was very sympathetic and understood we had no choice. I can't try to explain the shame I felt, one day I was the owner of a business, and the next; homeless, relying on handouts. One day I was driving a

Jaguar and the next an old Volkswagen polo called Flash.

We lived with mother-in-law for about two months, she never complained or fell out once, but it became unbearable because of Wendy's Christian sister. She had had her mother to herself throughout her childhood and now, when she was training to become a nurse, we had moved into her home. She never said much but made a point of ignoring us most of the time she was home and this made me feel very uncomfortable. Wendy also has a brother who regularly pleaded poverty for his family, he had twin boys, he did not work as he was on invalidity, but managed to smoke a fair amount of cannabis, how he got the money for this I don't know I can only guess it came unwittingly from his mother.

Thanks to our new doctor, who I christened Cairo Bill, Dr Rajan, we moved to an old rectory he had just bought and needed house-sitters, until he decided what he was going to do with it. He did charge us rent, but it was small, so we moved, we applied for a council house, we were lucky to get one, but where. Near Caerphilly, THE ROCK!

Graig-Y-Rhacca. Placed on the side of a hill overlooking Caerphilly, an idyllic spot for what could have been a very pleasant place to live but what a place, there was rubbish everywhere, three piece suites in the gardens, burnt out cars, boarded up houses, litter everywhere. It was the pits, the people on the whole were very nice but out of four hundred plus houses you could count the decent ones on the fingers of two hands. The rest were either unemployable or con artists who acted like the mafia and gave the impression they ruled the estate. The local shops had steel shutters on the front and most days the shutters stayed down and only the doors would open for fear of smash and grab raids. The children on the whole were out of control and had no parental guidance, the police would not venture into the site after dark for fear of attack. Junkies ruled, drug pushers were so in abundance you could fall over one anytime you turned a corner and it was a joy riders paradise, cars were stolen and set on fire every night. I think out of all the people I came into contact with, it was the unemployable I could not take to, the attitude that the world owed them a living made me very cross.

It's a sad fact of life that there are those who choose to spend their lives on the unemployable register. I use the term unemployable as they can't afford to take a job, they would be worse off financially.

The most important items in life, Sky television, cigarettes and booze, what sort of society have we created? It's a fact of life we have a lost generation and it will manifest itself in later generations, as the children follow the parents into the same life pattern.

I had never experienced anything like this and it wore me down so badly I could not cope with it. I had part time jobs driving for a local trucking firm, which helped keep my sanity as I was not at the Rock all the time I was up the road and only home two or three nights a week. Although Wendy and Kirk were there seven nights a week, I don't know how they managed it.

During this period I started writing to newspapers. I had never experienced such degradation, the filth and none caring attitude of the people, save a few who did try to get thing improved shocked me beyond belief. It seemed everyone was either on the fiddle, claiming dole, working on the side or on invalidity benefit but working anyway. I became paranoid about the site. I used to walk around taking photographs of this place but was warned off by the local mafia who thought I was working for the DSS. It got so bad at one point that I would only go out to get the daily paper.

WORK SHY

I can't afford to work you see,
It is a crying shame
I'd love to be in employment,
But I just can't play the game
My rent is paid, and my poll tax too,
And kids eat free at the school
I smoke and drink and play pool,
And I study to fiddle the rules.

Unemployment is my game,
When I sign on I print my name
I never had much education,
Although it's paid for by the nation
School for me held no attraction,
Skiving off was the big attraction
I teach my kids to fiddle and nick,
And on the dole they must stick.
So don't you think so bad of me
It is the system can't you see
So if you want to change the rules
You must replace political fools.

I once wrote to a major south Wales newspaper suggesting that when the national stadium wasn't being used, (the national stadium being the Millennium Stadium in Cardiff.) Could we not have a flog a yob day, you know, with all the trappings, hot dogs, funny hats, samba bands, etc.

I also suggested that the names of the ones to be flogged should be posted on the giant scoreboard, along with the offender's address and what his/her offence was. The idea was they should be led in, paraded around, then votes should be cast, and depending on votes the punishment meted out. The offender, after the punishment had been administered would be made to walk out all alone.

I fully expected a very hostile response but every phone call I got, and there were many, all agreed and offered their services to help set it up, alas nothing ever came of it, pity...

A few years later while recounting the story to a friend of mine who is a vehicle examiner, Mike Jenkins, he is one as I would say 'of the old school' you know the ones, beat them, flog them, send them back, we were talking about youth and the problems that we face with them.

The usual comments were made, flog the little bastards, that's all they understand, this bought on a lot of different comments from the group assembled. Who would do the floggings? 'I would,' said Mike. I then inquired what qualifications he would need to carry out such a task. 'None,' came the reply. 'I am the only one working here with letters after my name.'

At this I asked, 'what letters?'

'Well,' he said, not pausing for breath or thought, 'I've got one for fighting, one for abusive language, and one for threatening behaviour and if I get one more I will be looking for another job. So if a flogging job ever comes up it would suit me down to the ground.

FLOG A YOB

What an entertainment Saturdays would be
At the national stadium but no rugby shall we see
All the bands are playing, hot dogs are on sale
Samba bands beat on the drums, all the seats are free.

Crowds they will be cheering, excitement fills the air
As the yobs are led out one by one and tied into a chair
The names are on the scoreboard and their home address
The yob is looking round and breaks into a sweat.

The flogger marches in amid a roaring cheer
The cat of nine tales swishing, I bet he's had a beer
He waves to all the gathered crowd and looks at this poor yob
Then with a swish and a smile, he gets on with his job.

I know it's wishful thinking, the action for to take
It may be just the answer, to society we make
Our human rights prevent it, a pity all you cry
But as things are getting worse, it may be worth a try.

I had a job with a local trucking firm for a while, then I had an accident in my truck when a motorcycle ran into me. This cracked me up and I did not work for a long time. You often hear that people who have serious accidents dream of the incident for a while after, I still dream of this quite often.

I suffered from depression and the term everyone uses; 'stress' and had to attend the outpatients of the local psychiatric hospital for several months for treatment. I thought, 'this is the end', and for the second time in my life I felt like ending it all. I was taking Tamazapan and all sorts of other junk. I felt as if I was in a dream world most of the time and felt very tired and very bad tempered.

One day during a row with Wendy I told her to get off her arse and look for a job, this she did. She showed what a strong person she was. I had never seen this side of her, she started to train as a financial advisor. This took her away on courses for days at a time and I was left to look after Kirk. I became a househusband and took on the task of cooking and cleaning; this was not easy.

HOUSEWORK

I just can't stand it anymore, the constant sweeping of the floor
The dishes that are piled so high, the Fairy Liquid oh so mild
The scrubbing of the kitchen floor, the muddy footprints by the door.
The dirt it makes me feel so wild, my family says it's in my mind.

All the time it takes to clean and make the windows glint and gleam
I could be in some foreign land, on holiday on golden sand
But I know that's not for me, cleaning time spent by the sea
I should be home my mop in hand, not flaunting in some foreign land.

When all my cleaning it is done, I may just sit out in the sun
Watching birds as they fly by and see the clouds high in the sky
But as you know it's never done, to idle time in having fun
Much better then I hear you murmur, to hear the strains of the Hoover.

I must go now back to my labours, or I won't be granted any favours
The washing it has not been done and all the beds need turning down
The dusting it takes so long ornaments must be moved along
And at the ending of each day, make notes of what's to follow.

I decided that I could not go on the way I was I was relying on the drugs to get me through the day and sometimes taking more than I should, so I stopped taking all the medication. This was not easy, I had heard the term cold turkey and thought it was an excuse given so as not to give up drugs; it is no excuse. I felt worse for a long time but having Kirk to look after helped me. I finally got myself together, thanks to Kirk and Wendy for their support, I was acting like a real bastard.

I started a business again, for want of a better word, with a neighbour who had when we first came to the Rock showed us a welcome, probably veiled but at that point any friend no matter how flash was a welcome voice in a void of what I deemed to be a disaster area.

The business was pyramid selling, we would buy items as samples, distribute the samples to agents and get agents to sell them on at house party basis, then we would order any items that were sold at these house parties, deliver them, collect the cash and pay the agent a commission, which was not too much, so we kept the profit. This went quite well for a time. We even sold none alcoholic wine door-to-door and were snowed under with orders, some of our customers were even getting drunk on this fizzy plonk. I then fell out with my partner's wife, she was a grabbing bitch and that was that.

SO EASY

You never really see the fool he is so full of guile
He offers you this great big deal while on his face a smile
It's bound to make you millions he offers with a quip
And all it going to cost you is just a hundred quid.

You look into this deal of his and get this money greed
So your parted from your hundred quid and then set out to deal
But when you sit and think of this money making scam
You realise just what you've done so who's the silly ham?

So when you're offered deals so good millions for to make
Ask yourself this question should this chance I take
If the deal is guaranteed you're fortune for to make
Why is the guy that's selling it only wants a hundred quid?

Wendy did not trust him from the start, but he did show me friendship when I needed a friend. I think why Wendy did not like him was he always wore dark glasses, he never showed his eyes. Wendy was always suspicious of people who wear sunglasses all the year round, winter or summer, day or night. Why don't they show their eyes, is it because they lie so much and are afraid to show them for fear of giving themselves away? Eyes are a dead give away when someone is trying to con you, they may establish eye contact with you, but do they tell the truth? So if you can't see them how are you to know?

Each day I pass a girls' school, it's a preparatory school for young ladies, and as such its costs, per term, are huge. A main road divides the school, so each day young ladies of various ages have to cross the road to change classes.

The crossing is manned, it is traffic light controlled but the controller presses the button to change a set of lights in order for the young ladies to cross. The same controller has been operating the lights for fifteen years. He is short, white haired, always wears sunglasses, winter or summer, he never smiles or speaks to the pedestrian traffic, he just looks, so it seems, straight ahead. Does he have dark secrets to hide, or is it my imagination?

SECRET

Who can tell what secret thoughts lie behind those shades
Eyes that you cannot see, hidden from your gaze.
Looks that can't be analysed, or taken into trust
Because the wearer of the shades, is secretly in lust.
The looks that never reach you, because of darkened eyes
Will never gain the trust of people passing by.

Secret thoughts of darkened eyes are often very cold
Crooked deals and con tricks, lurking in their souls.
So watch out for the shaded ones, who hide behind the shades
The thoughts they hide are sinister, so just avoid their gaze.

Wendy deals in financial services at which she is extremely successful. She had to study very hard and in most ways took control of the situation we now found ourselves in. I on the other hand, went through a period of depression, I think it was not being in control, after all I had been in control for a long time. Then all of a sudden I was not in control of anything, not even my own destiny. There seemed to be no way forward, so Wendy went out to work and I stayed behind closed doors. I became a househusband. If anyone ever tells you that housework is easy they are strangers to the truth. That was when Wendy's mother died.

Juanita

Juanita was Wendy's mum, she fell down the stairs one day and broke her leg. While she was in hospital she was diagnosed with cancer, we were all very shocked, we all expected her to go on forever. I can see her now with her cup of black coffee and cigarette watching her favourite program: Taggart.

Juanita, was such a quiet lady, but alas a slave to those who took advantage of her good nature. Joan as she was known would see the good side of everybody, she was so laid back but if ever you crossed the line she would soon let you know you were on dangerous ground. She had held the family together since 1966 when she lost her husband Graham, he was killed in New York harbour, close to the Bayonne Bridge, in the Kill Van Kull channel, he was the Captain of an oil tanker. He was coming into harbour with a cargo of Naphtha from Karachi. Naphtha was the substance added to petrol in the sixties, the advertisements used to say put a tiger in your tank, Naphtha was the tiger.

His ship the 11,232 ton *Alva Cape*, loaded with 143,000 barrels of Naphtha, was in collision with the 16.000 ton U.S Tanker, *Texaco Massachusetts*, the accident was between Staten Island and New Jersey. They collided causing the Naphtha to spill out onto the sea, a tug tried to force the vessels apart but the Naphtha gas was sucked into the engine of the tug and a huge explosion took place. Most of the crew were lost.

It was found and proven that the pilots, these are employed by the Port Authority to ensure safe passage of shipping, both of the *Alva Star* and *Texaco Massachusetts,* were at fault and no blame was attached to the skippers on either ship, although it was later reported that the pilot on the *Texaco Massachusetts* was the one responsible for the collision.

Wendy was sixteen when this happened in the middle of her school exams. She worked hard to pass these exams, which only goes to show what a strong willed person she is. She has since been to see where the accident took place. I think this trip helped to lay a ghost to rest, as she did not know the full story until then, this was some thirty years later.

Wendy has a brother and sister, both younger than her, but they don't seem to need her since their mother died, maybe it's me they don't like, personally I don't give a shit. They leeched on their mother when she was alive and I am sure they are both suffering from guilt, that's why they don't keep it touch with Wendy. I know it hurts her but she hides it well and pretends it does not matter, but I know it does.

When her mother died we inherited a clock, and a plant we call Juanita, the clock chimes both hours and half hours, but since we acquired the clock it has not once chimed correctly. It strikes thirteen sometimes, we have never been able to get it right. I tell everyone it is just like Wendy's mum, unpredictable and surprising.

We left the rock behind us and bought a house in Caerphilly. I was working as a process server for local solicitors and doing a little private investigation work, this was very interesting work and it got my confidence back. All went well for a while but the jobs were thin on the ground so I went to work for Securicor, guarding sites, why I did this I do not know maybe it was the uniform.

The guarding job was a desperate existence. Twelve-hour shifts, you could be on a building site or in an office or, as I was at one time, at the Western Mail and Echo, this is where you do begin to see the other side of life. You suddenly become invisible, it's a strange feeling, I could walk through a room full of people working at computers and telephones and never be seen, nobody took the slightest notice. It was a crap job, so I went for an interview as a store detective, this was even worse and I got the sack because I never caught anybody. I could see them nicking clothes and such like from the store, I felt sorry for most of them and did not have the heart to put them through the trauma we were told to exercise. I was out of a job again.

GUARD

I think I may go crazy, at this new job of mine
It takes no brains to do it; it just takes up your time
The pay it is atrocious, conditions are quite bad
You put your safety on the line, for a measly few quid.

Your clothes are all supplied to you, at no extra cost
Until you come to leave this job and then you suffer loss
All you do is walk all night, and this is very taxing
But if you get hit on the head, questions they are asking.

You're not to tackle them you see, robbers and the like
Your only weapon to deter, is shout and give them fright
But if your shout is not enough and they approach too far
Phone the law, your only hope and pray they have a car.

You're issued with equipment, of this you must take care
Self-protection is the word, so criminals beware
You may come here to do your worst, to rob and to steal
No problems you will get from me, I'm not allowed to deal.

You may be asking questions, of why we do this job
It's simple for to answer, there is no other work
But if the day ever dawns, when we get our worth
I bet a quid they give my job, to a camera and a smurf.

Wendy had worked her socks off, much as she had during the time her father was killed, and had established herself in the financial industry. She was on the verge of setting up her own practice, she really had worked very hard, taking all sorts of exams and attending training courses.

Kirk was starting to show how clever academically he was and it soon became apparent, he was university material, but we were still having the rows. I was to blame for this unsettled period and I know it upset the whole family, but the demons were still in my head. I felt everyone was either looking at me with distain or talking about me, and when this obsession gets into your mind there it stays.

I was at such a low point I was imagining things were going on behind my back and felt very insecure. It was the fear of losing everything again that caused the strain. I had had enough of this, I had to get back into work.

If you have never been in the position of trying to find work, when you have been out of the work place, so to speak, you will know how hard it is. You are either too old or over qualified, or not qualified enough. You know you can do almost any job you go after, but there is a further hurdle to get over, does your face fit? If it doesn't you don't get the job. No matter how depressed you get, the only way up is to keep trying. Friends fall away at an alarming rate. It is at these times you get to know just who your friends are.

I had to get myself back into the work place. I was taken on as a foreman driver with a small valleys company but due to the Japanese company we were working for, the job did not last too long, they were cutting back on staff so we were laid off. It was not long before they closed the whole factory and moved the production to Prague where the labour costs were a fraction of what they were in South Wales.

GIVE US A JOB

I cannot find any work you see, I am over qualified
I've written several letters, with all the same reply.
I'm sorry to inform you, successful you are not
Of course, we'll keep you on our files, in case we do get stuck.

I've written for all sorts of jobs, the list is quite complete
But in this modern market place, with computers, you compete.
Gone has all politeness, no feeling of regret
It sometimes feels you're just a fish caught up in a net

You start to doubt your confidence, ability all ceased
Days they never change for you and then they turn to weeks.
The weeks they pass and suddenly, it's been another year
With only part time work to do, you suffer from despair.

I know the work is out there, I want some for myself
I know I have so much to give, if given halve a chance.
I really don't want that much pay, though money's hard to get
It's just a job I'm after, to get some self-respect.

My wife's been very patient, she works so hard you see
While I stay at home and clean the house, and get us all our tea.
I have some part time work, that comes in now and then
But it doesn't fill my time up, or get us out of debt.

I must admit that anger comes creeping in my mind
When I see all the youngsters, wasting so much time.
Don't mess around with dead end jobs, just get an education,
Or you will end up just like me, jobless in this nation.

My age was forty-six that year, the scrap heap was for me
My future it was grim, there's not much left you see.
There is one thing that I am sure, I won't give up the fight
As long as I can give my best, I'm going to win all right.

I then went into large vehicle driver instruction and got a job with a small family firm based in Cardiff, they were really nice people the only problem was they would not invest into the truck training side of the business, or pay the rate for the job. I stuck with them for a number of years, and enjoyed the job very much, so much so that when I left I went to work for another company doing the same job at twice the money.

The wife of the boss of the first company was a night club singer and she was very good. To make herself more attractive she had cosmetic surgery to enhance herself, although she did not needed it, but vanity took over.

SOFT TO THE TOUCH

Two implants were the order to further a career
A pair so cute and rounded, for everyone to leer
She really didn't need them, for hers were quite all right
But she did it for her old man, for him to squeeze at night.

While at a dinner party, looking very pretty
She sat across the table from someone very witty
Leering at her wonders, his eyes he could not take
He asked, 'if you squeeze them do they spring back into shape?'

The table went so quiet, the husband looked so shocked
We all were waiting for him to give this chap a sock
But just to add to our delight, she answered with a smile
If you want an answer to that, you'll wait a long, long time.

Teaching people to drive trucks, brings me into contact with many different people, the cross section of characters I get are very amusing, but for all the humour truck driving is a very serious and responsible job. Trucks are the lifeblood of the country, they bring all the goods you need for your daily life, although 90 percent of the nation only see a truck, which is in the way. Unless you are a lorry driver, you tend to see trucks as a nuisance, they are something to get in front of. To the truck driver, they are a living, breathing part of their lives, the care and attention, lavished on them would make most wives and girlfriends and some boyfriends and husbands jealous. I have taught ladies and men and believe me ladies are far easier to teach.

I would like to be able to take every car driver out in a truck to let them see what truck drivers have to put up with from motorists who 'do not signal, drive in the centre lane of the motorway, speed up when being overtaken, cut you up when they overtake you, and lots, lots more.

If you can imagine a job that will land you in prison for trying to earn more money honestly then you have truck driving, with all the restrictions placed on drivers today, it is more and more difficult to earn a good wage driving

So, remember.   NO TRUCKS : NO FOOD

TRUCKERS

From all the meat that fills the pies, to all the clothes you wear
Don't forget the journey, it takes travelling from here to there
The people who decry us, when driving down the road
All the things that you possess, or eat is carried in our load.

We see your mad eyes flashing, and your fists do often shake
And the thoughts that you are thinking, as progress we try to make
But spare a thought for those of us who work the highway long
Without us at the steering wheel, you wouldn't last too long.

The empty shelves in supermarkets, the garages, no fuel
The clothes shops with no garments, you'll really feel quite cool
The children with no schoolbooks, there won't be any school
So when you see us on the roads, try to keep your cool.

Imagine life without, petrol, heating oil or coal
The cold nights in the forest, for wood to heat your soul
No drugs at the chemist, or medicines for cures
And most of all no socks, to wrap your freezing toes.

So spare a thought for the truckers that travel everywhere
Bringing you all your food to eat and the clothes you wear
The petrol for your motors and the pills for all your ills
And keep out of our bloody way, especially on hills.

Chapter Nine

Five people, who were very close to me died within a year, first was my mother's sister, her name was Georgina, we called her Geo. She had been struck down with rheumatoid arthritis at a very early age, she had not long been married to Roy, when she was struck down with this terrible illness. Roy was so devoted to Geo, he would have done anything for her and he did. They never had any children, more's the pity, they would have been good parents, they were married twenty years when Geo contracted cancer and died.

Roy, almost a year later, died of leukaemia, I think a broken heart brought it on.

Then mother's other sister, Lillian, died of a heart attack. The look on the faces of family who were left tells a tale, because as everyone does, they expected her to live forever. I will remember Lillian as an outgoing, happy person, she was game for anything and was totally devoted to her husband Les and her two sons Tony and Nigel. She kept her home spotlessly clean and there was always a welcome for all who called in for a chat and a cup of tea, but she smoked herself to death.

Then a very good friend of mine died of leukaemia, John Inskip, he had taken me under his wing when we had our business and helped by serving in the shop and giving advise. Wendy tolerated him but John thought the world of her. Then Jeremy fell off a ladder and died.

DOUBTS

It's sad to see your family go, everything seems wrong
The only thing that you can do, is pretend to be so strong
You start to count your blessings, look to the ones that are left
But the sorrow that you're feeling, lies heavy on your breast

You question your mortality and think who will be next
You see all the sad faces, all looking drawn and vexed
You try to cheer yourself up, and put on that brave face
And try to tell yourself, they've gone to a better place.

But somewhere deep inside yourself, you know that it's untrue
But when you're in the deepest night, you hope it's true for you
We all hope there's a heaven with angels flying round
But deep inside we really know; we lie beneath the ground.

Just to put a lighter note, on the theme of death, which I seem to have stumbled into.

Where I grew up in mid Wales there were two real town characters, both had very successful businesses. Lionel was a greengrocer, he was as round as he was tall and always had a smile and some kind words to say to whoever came into his shop.

The other character, Austin, was the local undertaker, who also ran a garage repair and petrol station. Austin was also there to lend an ear to anyone's problems and was probably the only honest councillor of his generation, a position he held for many, many years. Anyway, the years took their toll on both and as they grew older, so they became closer. Then Lionel took very ill and was taken into hospital, nobody expected him to come out. Austin was visiting him every day to cheer him up but to no avail, Lionel was not getting better, it was as if he had given up the fight.

At this realisation Austin took drastic measures, 'measures' being the operative word. He went to the hospital to visit and as he was sitting by the bed he said to Lionel.

‘Come on old friend, you’ll get better, give yourself a chance.’

Lionel answered back. ‘Its no good, I’m going, I can feel it, I’m not coming out of here except in my box.

At that point Austin took from his pocket a tape measure and began to stretch it out along the length of the bed, then across the width of the bed.

‘What the hell are you doing?’ asked Lionel, sounding somewhat shocked at his effrontery.

‘Well,’ replied Austin, ‘if that’s the way you feel, I had better get one ready for you.’

A few weeks later Lionel was out of hospital, feeling a lot better. Alas he died two years later.

Austin went on for a further ten years, telling the story of how he saved Lionel’s life. What lovely people they were.

Wendy thought it was time for a change. I was quite happy where I was but it was time to move, so we bought a new house off plan and had to wait for it to be built. Then our problems started all over again, the building seemed to take forever and we nearly lost the sale of our old house due to the incompetence of the builders. So we told them we were moving in on the 17th of December 2001, a day before our 25th wedding anniversary, doors on the house or not, they were still painting as we moved in.

Our new house overlooks Caerphilly on the side of the mountain a beautiful spot even in winter, although the wind does blow very hard. In the summer it is so warm and many hours are spent in the garden with glasses of wine and gin and tonic, with Fairport Convention and Willie Nelson playing on the stereo; bliss. The barbecue lit and long evenings just enjoying the company of neighbours and friends chatting away and putting the world to rights.

Wendy has taken over the garage for her office, so she has not too far to travel to work. I have to go over the mountain every morning, which takes ten minutes. Kirk lives and works in London, he is a forensic archaeologist.

When we moved into our new house we had to do a snagging

list, that is a list of faults, it took two years to remedy all the faults, yet another example of the modern day builders. Now for some very serious stuff.

Wendy has discovered Ikea, you know that Swedish home designer, goodness knows what ideas she will come up with in the future, it will probably mean work for me, you know flat packs, screws, glue.

HELP

Ikea has just come to town
To turn my world upside down
With packs so flat and not too light
They're bound to keep me up at night
With all those screws and little dowels
I'm bound to let of several growls
Why did Ikea come to town?
To turn my world upside down.

At about this time I was diagnosed with diabetes. Probably bought on by the stress of the new house, I was getting very tired and was continuously thirsty, this sometimes gave me the shakes and a cramp like pain in my stomach, so I went to the doctors and was sent for tests, this worried me for some time. I was X rayed and made to drink sweet liquid, then blood was taken, I had to sit in a room for an hour then more blood was taken. I was then told I was diabetic and had to attend a clinic where they put drops in my eyes that blinded me for a few hours. I was poked and tapped, weighed and told to lose weight, I spent a lot of time back and forth to the doctors, asking questions sometimes it was difficult getting in to see him.

The doctor's surgery. You know those places you go if you're lucky enough to get an appointment, before you actually die. Look around, while you study the magazine in your hand you know the one, *Bird Fanciers' Journal* or *Home Maker*, try to diagnose the ailments that each one waiting may be suffering from. The limpers, the twisted ankle brigade, who just about manage to stumble to a seat amid loud groans and much agonising, the asthma cases who wheeze their way in and almost collapse begging the receptionist to let them go first in case they die, the stomach cases with the constant belching and breaking wind, you can always pick these out, no one else sits by them for obvious reasons. The malingerers, a breed apart, they have got everything wrong, if they haven't got it on the way in, they have it by the time they leave.

Have you ever thought it strange that when you see the same people outside the surgery environment they are either trying to sell you something off a market stall, offering you a deal on roof repairs or running in a marathon for charity, one that usually gives them the bulk of the money. Hold on now, I hear you cry that's a bit strong, but is it? Have you ever really stopped and given a thought as to where you last saw that man who is trying to sell you double glazing?

Trying to see the doctor should be easy, but we still have a feeling of dread when having to make a visit, mind you, if you think about it, the dread comes from the doctor's receptionist. You know, the storm trooper guarding the consulting room with every sinew of her being. You get the feeling that she would rather kill you than let you see the doctor. She will demand to know everything about you; what the ailment is, how long you have had it, have you tried aspirin or soaking in a hot bath, what does the chemist say about it, and if you haven't seen a chemist, why not? Don't you think the doctor's time is valuable, why haven't you tried alternative medicine? When, and only when, she is entirely satisfied, she will if you are lucky, give you an appointment. Mind you, it may be for three weeks hence, by which time you could have recovered or have been cremated.

There is one sure way to get to see your doctor very quickly, tell the storm trooper that you need the doctor's signature, this will give the doctor cash in hand, before you have fully finished the sentence, the storm trooper has you by the scruff of the neck and standing in front of the doctor with the cash.

HEALER

Doctor, Doctor help me please
I have got some aching knees,
I know you're busy and time is short
Your guard dog almost had me caught.
To get to you it takes some skill
Your receptionist has looks to kill,
She gives us hell-asking questions
Almost like the inquisition.
Why don't you chain her to her chair?
I'm sure she doesn't have a care
I know that you she wants to please
But that doesn't help my aching knees.

UPS AND DOWNS

Life is pretty good you see, despite its ups and downs
So when you're feeling pretty low, just get off the ground
You'll be surprised what you can do, just give it a chance
No need to sit on the outside, get in and have a dance

We're not on earth forever, this tale were often told
So do yourselves a favour, before you get too old.
Do whatever you want to and don't hold back at all
Then when you've achieved your goal, you're ten feet tall

Remember you have one shot, to make it on this earth
So don't waste time thinking, give it all you're worth.
You may not make a million, or travel round the globe
As long as you are happy, you've done a pretty good job.

I have had so much fun doing all the variety of jobs I have done, all gave me some added life experience and bought me into contact with some fascinating people. My job training people to drive lorries never ceases to surprise me. The doctor tells us to exercise, do something to make your heart beat faster, do something each day that frightens you, well I turn up for work.

When I take on a new trainee, I have to check his licence and ask a few questions as to what he has driven. One question I ask is: 'Do you have any physical disabilities that I should be aware of?'

One candidate answered after a long pause: 'I only have one testicle.'

A couple of stories about people I have trained.

Graham told me of the time he was taken to court for racial discrimination and dangerous driving. The incident happened on a very dark, wet morning. Driving as we all know in heavy rain is hard enough, but if your windows are steaming up and your eyesight is not so good, it's even more difficult. This is the story, in his own words.

"I was driving to work, it was a dark, shit day, everything was going wrong, no milk for my tea was the first thing, then the dog wouldn't come in, I got soaked looking for him, the car had a flat tyre and I was late for work. I was driving up the road in reasonably light traffic as it was five-thirty in the morning. I was driving along listening to the radio when, all of a sudden I felt a bump on the front of the car and a rumble across the roof. I braked hard and got out of the car, I went to the front only to find a bicycle trapped under the car. My first thought was; 'what twat left that in the road?'

I was in the process of dragging it clear when I heard a groan from the rear of the car. I rushed round to find this guy lying in the road. When I asked him what he was doing there he said that I had hit the rear wheel of his bike and catapulted him over the car. He was a black guy dressed in black, not the easiest to see on such a morning. After helping him to his feet he insisted on calling the police, what I meant to say at that point was this. 'If you had been wearing something white I would have seen you', but it came out as 'if you had been white I wouldn't have hit you'. That's when I thought, 'now I'm in trouble'. £400 fine for driving with undue care and attention and six points on my licence. £250 for racial discrimination, £2,000 compensation. If only there had been milk for my tea.'

Peter was a pilot instructor who was finding it hard to pass his pilot's medical, so he decided to give up flying and to start driving for a living, so I taught him to drive a lorry. Peter was hired by an Arab sheik to deliver his new customised jet to Dubai. Peter's wife, who wasn't a good traveller, was persuaded to go for the trip. She was a bit reluctant but thought, 'well it's a chance to fly in a luxury jet', and luxury it was, fitted out in leather and gold trim; real luxury. They set off in this customised jet. Now Peter's wife, not knowing what weather they would encounter, had taken her new suede jacket, matching bag and shoes. These she wore to travel, she had in her handbag her passport and all the usual bits and bobs. About two hours into the flight she felt really ill and not being able to make it to the toilet, she quickly emptied out the contents of her handbag and was ill in the bag. She put all the documents and bits into the pockets of her jacket, closed the bag and fell asleep. Sometime later, they landed at Dubai, taxied the plane to the parking area and made their way to the customs control. Peter, seeing his wife wasn't feeling too good, took her jacket and bag off her, so she had nothing to carry. When they came to passport control, he asked her where her passport was, she said, not thinking too clearly, 'in my bag'. Whereupon Peter opened the bag and thrust his hand in before she had realised what she had said. I leave his comments to your imagination.

Travelling, has become very important to Wendy and I, whenever we get a spare week, which is not very often, away we go. I must say I do love to travel I never thought I would but to see other countries is such an experience I would recommend it to every one. My family never travelled except to the shops, sad.

I often feel whilst travelling to work on a morning when the sunrise is so bright and clear, I could go on driving forever. It's just a feeling that comes over me like someone is trying to take me where I would love to go, never again returning to the hum drum life that has been created in order to survive every week. Doing the work that will yield a modest pay packet, which is never enough, so I can start again the next week, life's merry-go-round, that never seems to get anymore exciting than the daily drive to and from work. WORK, what an awful word that is, it gives no inspiration, no light at the end of the tunnel, only a continuation of misery and stress. If only we could wave a magic wand and go and do what our heart desires, instead of what the bank manager wants us to, no mortgage to pay, no car to run, no bills to pay, only adventure and excitement.

Why do we have to toil all day
Only to collect a meagre pay
Running round chasing tails
Killing time biting nails.

Would we not get fed up after a while having no roots, no place to call our own, just hotels, room service and taxis. Just think how it would feel if you were not contributing to life in some small way. Even if it's giving a friend help when they need it, would they get the same help if you were not there?

You may change history in some small way. Would it happen if you were on permanent holiday? Ask yourself this question, "if a tree fell in the middle of a forest, and no one was there to hear it, would it make a noise?"

Since 9/11/02 I have taken the philosophical view, "what will be will be." Each morning I start my day with a drive into Cardiff, we pass over a flyover on the Gabalva interchange, in the distance the sun rises over a part of the city called Splott, each sunrise is different, the colours are always changing and I wish I could stop on that stretch of road to see all of the sunrises.

SUNRISE

Nothing can compare with a sunrise over Splott
Every day as dawn comes up, it's really got the lot
It makes you glad to be alive and bathes you in its calm
The rays that come across at you are like a soothing balm.

The colours bright and living, warm the city streets
It calms the darkness of the night and wakens us from sleep
A day has come to life again and who knows what it plots
Nothing can compare with a sunrise over Splott.

We all suffer from memory loss, not serious I hope, but things that have happened in my dim and distant past, which I don't think of, or remember, sometimes come into my head. I lie in bed unable to sleep because my mind will not shut down, I suffer from insomnia and find I sleep for a couple of hours then wake with memories and thoughts rushing through my head. How vivid these memories are, almost as if they happened yesterday, yet sometimes I can't even remember what I had for breakfast the morning before, that I must admit worries me a little. Have you ever driven through a village or town and not had any recollection of passing through them. I must admit it has happened to me on more than one occasion, once I even backtracked just to make sure I hadn't had an accident. I hadn't.

When I was five years old I was knocked off my three wheel trike, when I was discharged from hospital some weeks after the accident, I had no recollection of anything happening, yet forty-five years down the line I found myself waking up in the middle of the night in a cold sweat, re-living every moment. I can remember going down a hill, turning a corner and watching the pick up truck coming towards me, I can even feel the impact, it is a bit scary. I was not allowed another trike, a scooter took its place it was red, white and blue. I loved that scooter, it had big wheels with solid tyres, and a brake on the back wheel, which was operated by your heel. I called it 'Scotch Mist'. I don't remember why I called it that, but it was my pride and joy, I even took it into my bedroom at night after polishing it with an orange coloured polish my mother had purloined from her place of work.

Other things I thought I had forgotten often come into my mind, my first cigarette and how sick I was. I can remember exactly where I smoked it and the brand name, it was *Domino*, a small cigarette you could buy, there were only four in a packet, guaranteed to make you puke. Yet I can't remember who I was with when I smoked it, I find that strange.

Dreams, as well as memories, seem to re-occur, dreams of people long gone often haunt the few hours of sleep that I have, most of them are good dreams but some times they are very frightening, and I wake with a start unable to move, for a few moments thinking I am still asleep dreaming. I suppose it must be to do with subconscious thoughts or a guilty conscience. I should be analysed.

NO—SENSE

Memories of times that have long past
Which are keeping the bad things at bay,
Things that you did when you were at school
Past memories of long ago days.

We try to remember the things we forget
Or forget the thing we shouldn't
We remember the things we wouldn't forget
And forget all the things that we couldn't.

Always remember the times that you have
And the days will seem twice as long
But the worst thing my friend is to get to the end
Remembering things that went wrong...

Ghosts, not in the supernatural sense but ghosts of the past. Things that haunt you without letting go, like a memory that you would love to forget but can't, a film you saw that has left an impression on your mind, that you cannot erase, but every now and then comes into your subconscious and starts to trouble you again. A piece of music, a smell, the perfume of someone walking by that you may catch on the breeze, all these things can bring back the ghosts to haunt you. Places can have the same effect, have you ever been in a place for the first time and suddenly know your way around, this is commonly called déjà vu, that is to say you think you have been there before, but I think you may have been there in some previous existence. I know it sounds silly but there are some who fervently believe in there being another existence, there have been occasions where I have felt this very strange phenomenon myself.

Wendy, treated us to a few days in Rome, a city full of history and monuments, the most awe inspiring was without a doubt the Sistine chapel, the Michaelangelo painted ceiling, must be the most wonderful work of art in the world. I was so taken with it, not for its religious connotations, but for its sheer beauty and splendour. Maybe not the best words to describe it but they do it for me. I would go back again just to see it once more.

The Coliseum in Rome gave me a feeling of death, it was overwhelming and it made me cold and scared, it was so creepy. I could still hear and see the blood and gore of it, and I found the voices almost unbearable. I feel things, things that are long gone, sometimes I can't go into a building or place because of the violence and mayhem that took place there, also I feel sadness in some places, not for myself, but for those who went before me. When in Rome we went into a café at the foot of the Spanish Steps called Babbingtons tea rooms. While we were waiting for our tea, I saw a cat, a striped tabby cat, being a cat person I bent down to stroke it, but as I reached down the cat disappeared. When I asked the ladies who worked there where the cat had gone, they told me the cat, exactly as I described it, had died five years earlier. Ghost or what? The ladies were quite taken aback by my experience.

Travelling through certain parts of France, I can feel the hostility of war and I can picture myself running across fields. I feel a gun in my hand, I can feel the recoil as I pull the trigger and I can feel myself falling to the ground. 'What a load of bull', I hear you say, but believe me I do have these feelings. There are places I have visited that I cannot get out of fast enough and there have been a few First World War battlefields and cemeteries that I have found difficulty in going to because I can still feel the people who died and who are buried there.

FRIGHTS

Don't be afraid of bumps in the night
We all know they give a terrible fright
The steps we hear which sound on the stair
Everyone knows there's nobody there.

The creaking floorboards bumps on the roof
If there are ghosts then give us some proof
The ghosts in your mind are ones that are real
The fright that haunts is the ones that you feel.

But don't be afraid they are only dreams
So don't let them spoil all of your schemes
But if when you're gone you find another dimension
Please get in touch and I'll give it a mention.

My hobby, though some say it is a depressing subject although I find it fascinating, is the First World War. I have visited Belgium and northern France and walked the battlefields and visited the cemeteries and I'm not ashamed to say I cried. I cried for the total waste of life and the stupidity of MANKIND! I find myself asking the question everyone who has had some experience of war either on the home front or in battle asks: WHY?

I feel that the battlefields and cemeteries of Flanders and other theatres of war should be compulsory visits for all future generations, and if at any time it fails to move them, then ask those who fought in the war or lost a loved one for their opinion. During my life it seems there has been a war raging somewhere in the world all the time.

I wonder what I would have done had I been called up to fight? Could I have faced an enemy with a gun in my hand? I don't know, what I do know is that war is the last resort, I feel there must be a better way. War is not glamorous it's messy, it's horrific, it's final, it's the *end* of humanity, it will destroy us all if we let it.

I never experienced war and I will be eternally grateful for this. I don't think I could have faced the dangers that my father and grandfather had to face at such a young time in their life. I pray to whoever is supposed to be in control of our destiny that my children and grandchildren never have to suffer such horrors.

Compare what forces men and women went through in the two most horrific wars of modern times. They returned from active service and were expected to get on with their lives, today, service personnel have stress counselling and rehabilitation. I'm not saying they have it any easier, but there is more infrastructure in place to help them get back to some sort of normality though some never do. So, did we judge those old soldiers a little harshly when they suffered from such trauma for the rest of their lives? I think maybe we did, many a back was turned on the disabled and disfigured because mankind is not tolerant of anything that is not perfect .We don't, or can't, see the inner person, the one who is desperately seeking acceptance from the rest of us, we pretend those who are not perfect do not exist although the problems they have encountered could have been the result of defending us from a greater enemy.

When I first visited the battlefields of Beaumont Hammel on the Somme, I walked through the trench systems, my friend could not even get through the gates for the noise and cries of the soldiers. I did not feel this at that place but in later years, I visited lots of battlefields and there are some I can't go on to. I can't explain it; it's a cold sticky feeling, sort of claustrophobic. I do believe that something exists after we depart this world, that is to say that when we shed this mortal coil we don't come back as something else. If you believe in good you must also believe in evil, so if there is a God, there also must be a Devil. Sobering thought eh!

On a visit to the Imperial War Museum, I was so humbled by the stories of bravery and the paintings depicting battles and heroic feats of war. One painting that took my attention more than others was of soldiers who had been gassed with mustard and chlorine and had been blinded. Soldiers in tattered uniforms and covered in the filth of war stumbling along in a line, each with an outstretched hand resting on the shoulder of the man in front being led by a stretcher bearer to an aid station. In the background of the painting a football match was taking place. The painting is by John Singer Sargent, and is called, *GASSED*.

Both world wars had heroes, some who survived, some who did not. One real hero who always comes to mind for me was a young woman who was executed by the Gestapo during the Second World War, her name was Violette Szabo. A film was made of her life, it was called, *Carve Her Name With Pride*. It starred Virginia McKenna in the leading roll. The reason I mention this is to tell of the poem that was her code to authenticate her when she contacted England. It was written by a man called Leo Marks, it has no title and it is said that it was originally written for his girlfriend who was killed. I may be a bit soft but I carry these words with me in my wallet for me they are the most moving words I have ever read.

The life that I have is all that I have
And the life that I have is yours.
The love that I have for the life that I have
Is yours and yours and yours.
A sleep I shall have, a rest I shall have
And death shall be but a pause.
For the years I shall have in the long green grass
Are yours and yours and yours.

There are a lot of war poets and a lot of very moving words written on the subject, all will be familiar with Laurence Binyon. No? Well, when you read this you will, it is verse four of a poem. I think that words such as these must be written from the heart, but from a broken heart. I wish I could write such beautiful words

FOR THE FALLEN

They shall not grow old, as we that are left grow old
Age shall not weary them, or the years condemn,
At the going down of the sun, and in the morning
We will remember them.

I get a lump in my throat on Armistice Sunday, watching the old soldiers marching past the cenotaph. I can't help feeling very humble at such occasions and I must admit to a tear or two at the stories told by some of the survivors. They are the real heroes, the ones who put themselves against an enemy, not knowing if they are going to see the next sunrise or sunset. I have often asked myself could I do the same, and I must admit I don't know.

The reason I have got into this is one Saturday afternoon on a visit to mothers, I was looking through some old photos as I am trying to put together a family history so Kirk, my son, will know something of his family.

While looking through old dusty boxes I happened on a small wallet, in the wallet was folded a piece of paper. When I opened it there were two silver paper horseshoes and a poem written on the 13th of May 1943. Mother knew that the horseshoes came from her wedding cake, but she had never seen the poem, so I am going to include it but make no claim to it at all. It was written by A. J. Bowmaker, I don't know if he was on my father's ship during the war or not, but here is his poem.

Farewell to our section, Farewell to the north
To office and factory, the best place on earth,
To work takers, bookkeepers, plant workers too
Here's wishing all the best and good luck to you.

No more will the corridors sound with your song
Nor the clocks gaily ring as you hurry along,
And bustle and chatter will all pass away
When we change to the south on the fifteenth of May.

No more will we see the trucks on the roads
With the truck drivers trucking their various loads,
There'll be no sign of life but the rabbits and sheep
And what was once active will now be asleep.

We'll miss the stone shops with their background of green,
Assembly and charge offload magazine;
The stillages working in shop thirty-three
Will all now be silent and dead as can be.

We'll have no more meals in the old north canteen
And concerts and pictures will no more be seen;
No more will we listen to "any prohibited"
As we pass through the gate with our passes exhibited.

No class distinction, one big family all
No shirking our duty we answered the call;
So goodbye to the north we've enjoyed our stay
For again duty calls and we must obey.

There's been to our view a black wreath displayed
That we are "killed in action" but are not dismayed,
No matter how rumour or fate on us frown
We might now "be dead", but we'll never lie down.

13 / 5 /1943 A. J. Bowmaker

I get very worried about the way we seem to have evolved as a human race, we are supposed to be sympathetic, forgiving and caring. Where have we gone wrong?

Persecution still goes on, we allow it to continue, we have a right to live our lives in peace and quiet, but there are tyrannical regimes that will not allow people to enjoy this basic human right. I have learned about the persecution of people from newsreels and newspapers. Maybe I have a limited and possibly tunnel view about persecution. The most horrendous was the Holocaust. We read, or see through old newsreels, what human beings were subjected to. I can only imagine what suffering they went through. To try to understand the fear and dread is almost impossible for those of us who live in this modern society.

Six million Jews; men, women and children were systematically exterminated, murdered, tortured and abused by a regime that seemed to survive on the suffering of others. What kind of human beings could dream up such horrendous tortures, what went through the minds of those who carried out such atrocities? How did they live with the pictures that must have remained in their heads and what did all this murder achieve? Adolf Hitler and Stalin are to be listed among the worst, murdering millions of their own people.

Ethnic cleansing carried out in my life time in Vietnam, Cambodia, the Congo, Zimbabwe, Croatia and Bosnia, Tiananmen Square, remember Idi Amin, Pol Pot, Slobodan Molosovitch, Sadam Hussein and closer to our home Northern Ireland. What sort of people are these that do such horrendous things to their fellow human beings? How does God allow this to happen? That is if there is a God, not that I am doubting his existence, but you would think if there was a God he would stop all the madmen from committing these atrocities. The question should arise, if any person has to torture their fellow human being in order to stay in power, would it not be better for all concerned for this person to be taken out of power? Not necessarily killed, but imprisoned for the rest of there natural life, in the same conditions as their victims. Would this not make more sense rather that kill them? Let them suffer a fate worse than death, lock them up and throw away the key.

We live in a society that thrives on greed, violence, persecution and torture, child abuse and slave labour, but what are we doing about it? Sod all.

Remember when Martin Luther King and John Lennon were murdered? And how humankind had just taken a step backwards when Steve Beko was murdered in South Africa, Steven Lawrence was murdered in London. When Nelson Mandela walked free from Robin Island. I wonder if his book, *Long Walk To Freedom*, was in his mind at that moment. The iron curtain coming down, what a celebration that was and what people thought when Rudolf Hess died in Spandau prison. London's notorious Cray twins, Myra Hindley, Ian Brady, the Yorkshire ripper, the Black Panther and Ian Huntly. The Hungerford massacre all these events; have affected us all in different ways. So ask yourself this one question: WHY.

I have included some of my war poetry although I have never experienced war I have tried to put my feelings into words.

GOING HOME

Lying in a shell hole, wounded and in pain
Blood is flowing freely, as the pouring rain
Mud and filth surround him, bullets whizzing by
He lies in his would-be grave, none to hear his cry

The wound it hurts like fire, burning hot like coal
He prays for some deliverance, for his wounded soul
Why did he get shot, he thought he would be safe
But when the bullet hit him, he fell flat on his face

Sliding down this slimy hole, amongst the long dead
Those who went before him, skulls that once were heads
Staring with great wide grins, holes that once were eyes
Did they live at all he asks, with homes, kids and wives.

He lies with ghosts around him, in his hole of mud
And listens to the shellfire, and tries to stem the blood
It's getting dark and colder now, will he see the dawn
His mouth is dry, aching head, bleeding has slowed down.

Star shells burst above him, lighting up the sky
Bullets less, as time goes on, darkness fills his mind
Cries of pain from no man's land, drifting on the breeze
He cries aloud with all his strength, help, help please.

Hours have now passed by him, all he feels is fear
He doesn't want to die alone, not here, not here, not here.
He sees his mother's image, he cries to her in vain
Help me mother, he cries out, take away this pain.

Blackness then surrounded him holds him in its dark
Darkness is so comforting, it takes away the stark
He feels that he is floating, high above the ground
Looking down on no man's land, corruption all around.

Can you hear me, please wake up, open up your eyes
The nurse who looks down on him, angel from the sky
Hello old son, how do you feel? You're a lucky chap
Stretcher bearers found you, you had a nasty tap.

We had to take a leg from you, just below the knee
So you're going home tomorrow, back to rest and ease
It's hard to lose a part of you, in that land of slime
Lucky though he is alive not trapped in war's cruel time.

LEE ENFIELD

My best friend is Lee Enfield, always by my side
He helps me out in times of stress, he never ever lies
He is so true and powerful, always gets the mark
My best friend is Lee Enfield, in daylight or in dark.

We march together up the line, singing out so loud
We sleep together every night, on the cold hard ground
I feel so brave just having him, hanging on my arm
When he speaks its always loud, he has no hint of charm.

My best friend is Lee Enfield, I use him every day
Doing what he does best, he helps me earn my pay
To keep him clean is such a task, with all mud and slime
But when he's clean he's perfect, working every time.

They told us back at training camp, never lose your friend
Get to know him inside out, and keep him close at hand
Always keep him loaded, and spare clips in your pack
He's the best friend you'll have, come the big attack.

GRANDPA

Grandpa sat upon a bin in the corner of the shed
His hands were strong his face was kind, a hat upon his head
His age was nearly eighty, but his eyes they were still bright
He sat upon that dirty bin and watched us work that night.

That night while we were working, thunder filled the air
Lightning flashed and thunder crashed, with noise to rent the air
As I looked across the shed, where old grandpa sat
His head was forward on his chest, and on the floor his hat.

I looked across at this old man, his hands upon his lap
And made a move towards him, to pick up his old hat
The man who worked beside me, held me back just then
Let him sleep, he's all right, it happens now and then.

He said it started in the war, we call it Grandpa's sleep
He was very badly shelled, when he fought at Ypres
The bombs, as thick as flies, came raining down on Ypres
So since that day when thunder sounds, grandpa takes a sleep.

When Grandpa woke, his eyes did flash, he looked up to the sky
It was the look of someone lost, and tears they filled his eye
We pretended not to notice, the look on Grandpa's face
And as we all resumed our work, we knew he missed his mates.

So when a thunderstorm is on, remember you this rhyme
And think of all those soldiers, marching up the line
And spare a thought for Grandpa, and his bin still in the shed
He doesn't sleep there anymore, he marches at their head.

IN THE MINDS OF SOLDIERS

To see no more the world in light
To be forever in darkest night
The images of comrades dead
All inside my aching head.

When this war is over and done
Will we remember our missing sons?
Or will those with eyes who cannot see
Be the only ones with vision.

If you could only see the sights
That come to haunt me in the night
The limbless that always smile, so bright
The sightless that see only night.

The shell-shocked that never sleep at night
The dead who are no more
Of bombs and guns, wire and gas
The trenches that are deep and vast.

The big guns all lie rusting now
No more to make, there dreaded row
No creeping barrages to lay
They all lie silent here today.

The gas, the bombs, they are no more
The guns are lying on the floor
The fighting man, he fights no more
He's gone home to his children.

CENOTAPH

Reminders that are stark and cold
The stone heart never beats
The rifle pointed to the ground
Statues stare at feet.

Hands folded at the front
Eyes that look so still
Reminders of forgotten wars
On every village hill.

Poppies on the eleventh day
At eleven in the morn
All the poppies in the world
Won't heal the hearts war torn.

The tears for a fallen pal
Fill every soldiers eye
Some will stare at the ground
Others stare at sky.

The memories from yesterday
Seem very real to them
Buried in some foreign land
The friend from far off days.

Lets tend the cenotaphs
Keep them clean and bright
For every day we may have
The dead have only night.

TALLER

They sent me home without my legs
I left them back in France
No more will I go walking
No more for me to dance
I don't know where they're buried
Somewhere on the Somme
I wonder will I get them back
When I'm dead and gone.

Or will I stay upon these wheels
Controlled with just my arms.
They tell me I'll have wooden legs
Much better than my own
I'd like to be much taller
I hope this will be done
Just to stand upon some legs
When I face my mum.

TAFFY

Taffy was a Welshman
Taffy had sore feet
Taffy took a number nine
On the road to Ypres.

Taffy dug some trenches
Taffy had no sleep
Taffy shot a German
Serving up in Ypres.

Taffy caught some shrapnel
Taffy went down weak
Taffy got an ambulance
Coming back from Ypres.

MARK

Get the cross upon the mark,
Squeeze the trigger slow,
Watch the bullet hit its mark,
Watch the life just go,

Look out for another mark,
Keep so still and low,
Never leave a telling mark,
As you hide out in your hole,

Another target get the mark,
Looking through the sights,
Slowly now get the mark,
Just snuff out a life,

I wonder will I be a mark,
Who will sight at me,
I hope it's quick on the mark,
And I can go to sleep.

MISERY

Bully beef and biscuits, petrol tasting tea
This is all the Tommy gets every day to eat
Cold and wet all around, most have trench feet
If only they could get some grub, good enough to eat.

A tot of rum to help them, into no man's land
Whistles blowing, there is no time to stand
A bullet in the back, if they fail this last command
Bullets bouncing off the trench into bags of sand.

Good luck the cry goes out to fall on deafened ears
A scramble forward, hundreds go, not many will return
Those who do ask again, when will they ever learn
Many brave were lost, good men of so few years.

When this war is over who will push the plough?
Who will gather all the corn? Who will reap and sow?
Who will be the father of generations yet to come
When all the young men are scattered on the Somme.

THE TRAIN

Platforms filled with sulphur smoke
Trains are full with fighting folk
Wives and lovers anxious stand
Clasping at the fighters hands.

Off to fight this dreaded foe
All these fighters so boldly go
Never showing nerves or fear
Though all who stay shed a tear.

These heroes who will risk life
Leave behind a love or wife

Never thinking of the worst
Positive thought must come first.

Wives and lovers meet for tea
With letters from the battlefield
Censored mail from foreign parts
Words to warm a saddened heart.

Platforms filled with sulphur smoke
Welcome home those fighting folk
Wives and lovers searching crowds
Finding heroes walking proud.

Trains that no more our heroes take
Keep them home and keep them safe
All the platforms quiet now
Away from war's crash and row.

SOMME

Somme is where the fighting was
Somme has trenches full of gas
Somme where killing bullets fly
Somme where all the soldiers die.
Somme has rats as big as dogs
Somme has roads made of logs
Somme has nurses very brave
Somme has thousands in a grave.
Somme had some who did return
Somme has generals who never learn
Somme will never walk again
Somme are carried from the train.
Somme have not returned at all
Somme will lie just where they fall
Somme will visit battlefields
Somme has poppies red and real.

Somme is hiding lots of dead
Somme is flooded with blood so red
Somme is where cenotaphs stand
Somme should never war again.

MOUTH ORGAN

Someone nicked my mouth organ
I bet it was the Hun
He pushed us out of our trench
He had us on the run.

He crept upon us one dark night
Further down the line
We ran like hell to save our lives
We left our kit behind.

We took the trench back again
We had an awful fight
We took it in broad daylight
Not in the dead of night.

The Hun put up a cracking fight
Before we pushed them back
But my mouth organ was missing
It's in some Hun's knapsack.

RATS

Here they come again, sniffing all around
Those big brown rats, sniffing at the ground
Searching for an easy feast of anybody dead
I'd like to take a shovel, and beat them on the head.

The rats are just as big as cats, feeding on the dead
Snuffling and screeching, torments in your head
Brazen as a robber, they steal all you have got
Sleep in your foxhole and bite holes in your socks.

Your sleep is interrupted, what little sleep you get
Rats come creeping in, no matter how snug you get
They smell of death, slink around, tearing at the dead
Too fond of meat these rats are, to even look at bread.

Fire is the answer, burn the blighters out
See them burning, screaming, running all about
Hurling into no man's land, burning as they go
Hundreds of them petrol soaked, make a terrific show.

DICK V.C.

Crippled Dick walked with a stick
So everyone thought he was thick
They would laugh and poke fun
Didn't know he was shot with a gun

Kids in the street would shout at Dick
Why can't you walk without your stick
They would always scream and shout
Come and chase us you silly trout.

Then one day as sharp as a pin
Dick was summoned to the king
A medal bright and shiny new
On Dick's chest for all to view.

Now when Dick walks with his stick
All the kids beside him skip
No more fun at him they take
Proud to help and call him mate.

POPPIES

It's quiet on the western front
Now the shelling it has stopped
The Kaiser's men are walking home
Across a corrupted muddy Somme.

This field of death and hatred
Which bears the scars of war
Should never more be wakened
By men and guns and war.

Dead will rise from time to time
Bleached bones in the sun
Just look at man's dreadfulness
And bones that once were sons.

Tell you children of this place
Bring them here to see
The horrors of the western front
And poppies in the fields.

BULLY BEEF

We found a tin of bully beef, Chalky White and me
Lying on the ground in no man's land underneath a tree
With bullets flying all around, shells as thick as soup
We dived into a shell hole for shelter and re-group.

We had not eaten for three days hunger filled our soul
Here we were in no man's land stuck in that great hole
We had to have that bully beef no matter what it cost
For if some others came along we knew it would be lost.

Chalky crawled out of the hole through the slimy goo
Slowly edging near the prize a thought of real food
What a find old Chalky said as he reached out at the tin
It was a jerry booby trap; it blew him limb from limb.

LETTERS HOME

Letters home the sergeant called we go at five am
Give them to the corporal he will send them on
Remember not to mention exactly where you are
You know the censor's pencils are always very hard.

Tomorrow is the big push we'll send this jerry home
So try to get a bit of sleep at daybreak we have rum
Clean your kit and rifle make sure your bayonet's sharp
And first thing in the morning jerry will need his harp.

Dawn came up so misty, our eyes were full of sleep
A silence oh so eerie a great shuffling of feet
All along the line the rum tot jug was passed
Throats as dry as burned toast gagged at this repast.

Waiting for that whistle a lot of us were ill
The captain looking at his watch standing very still
A bird sang out in no man's land maybe it's all over
The whistle blows its shrill cold call we go up and over.

Bullets swishing all around from the jerry guns
We were told to walk across but we started into run
We found a bit of cover and dived into a ditch
Men were being mowed down, bullets swish, swish, swish.

Hundreds of our brave men fell on that sad day
Strewn about no man's land like freshly mown hay
We took the trench jerry held, costs were very high
We send a lot of jerrys to play harps high in the sky.

LICE

The bullets and bombs they would kill us
The trench foot was a terrible thing
The food when we got it was awful
But the lice would send you insane.

I'm sure they were trying to eat us
Each night as we rested our head
For if we didn't have them in clothing
We bloody well had them in bed.

They itched to drive a man crazy
They were in all your sensitive parts
You scratched and twisted all ways
They even nested in your old socks.

Clearing them out was called chatting
Not talking or telling of dreams
Burning them out with a candle
By running the flame up the seams.

They laid eggs by the thousand
Impossible to clear out the lot
Some men they drove them crazy
I'm sure some were glad to get shot.

Spraying with creosote killed them
But when you got dressed in your kit
The creosote leeched and caused blisters
As big as a one penny bit.

We suffered a lot from the Jerry
We suffered a lot from the food
Our feet were as sore as they could be
But the lice could have won this Great War.

FINGER

Creeping out in no man's land
Spying out trenches at night
I came across this finger
It gave me a terrible fright
I stared at this handless finger
Just pointing in darkest night
I wondered who could have lost it
Imagining what it's owner was like
This finger was pointing at jerry
All alone in that terrible place
Just waiting for it to be buried
And to claim it's own little place.

DESERT

We used to like the beach and roll in soft gold sands
Building castles digging holes feel it in our hands
Sandwiches and ice cream crunch with every bite
We wish we were back there not here in this deadly fight.

The desert is not friendly it will kill you if it can
Not like the sands of Devon and its ice cream van
No joy for man this wasteland no cooling breeze for us
Instead we dodge the bullets fired straight at us.

Patrols they are a nightmare heat to burn our skin
The flies and bad conditions stinking latrine bins
The heat and sweat kill appetites, nights are freezing cold
I hope this war will end soon before we all grow old.

We hate this bloody desert and all it crawling tics
Scorpions and lizards the constant smell of shit
Rats you could put saddles, on that eat the dead at night
We hear them gnawing on our mates to give us all a fright

If ever I get home alive I'll not come back again
I be a bloody conchie and serve time in a cell
To ask a bloke to live like this is a bloody sin
So get us from this hell on earth back to our own kin.

EASE

Our dugout was our hiding place a sanctuary from war
It protected us from shelling and from our sergeant's roar
The door was just a blanket, the floor was sticky mud
Water leaked in through the roof often stained with blood

The air was never fresh it smelt of bombs and death
Rats would come at mealtime and steal whatever's left
We hit them with our rifles and stab them with our knives
The rats of Somme kept coming with shining bloody eyes.

Trench foot was a problem and dry feet a luxury
Water poured it filled the trench slimy blue and green
Our uniforms were filthy with mud and lice and fleas
Our dugout was the refuge where we took our ease.

STRETCHER-BEARER.

We wait in front line trenches until we hear the call
Stretcher bearer, stretcher bearer, then our blood runs cold
We scramble over the parapets and run toward the shout
If we're very, very lucky we get the poor sods out.

I have survived the bullets and dodged the flying shells
Although I've had three partners who did not do as well
The first was cut in half by a splintered shell
He never stood a dog's chance I hope he's not in hell.

The second one, a nice chap lost a leg below his knee
I felt the blast that got him, the shell it flew past me

I carried him towards our lines and hoped he would not die
The sounds I will remember were his agonising cries.

The third one was a Cockney by Bow bells he was born
A strong and willing giant that treated war with scorn
He'd bellow at the Hun and curse the slimy mud
He was mown down when bullets hit him thud, thud, thud.

I have another partner now just a lad of seventeen
He lied to get into this war of horrors never dreamed
He thought war was glorious and never thought of death
Sights he's seen, cries he's heard make him gasp for breath.

I hope we both survive this place but the chances are so slim
Perhaps my turn will be next or perhaps it will be him
Whatever way it goes I hope what I have done
Will send some poor unfortunate back home to his mum.

ROSES

They called them the roses of no man's land
Those angels of mercy with fair tender hands
They came to the front with healing charms
To help with the wounded that carried arms.

The sights they saw would haunt their dreams
To wake in the night still hearing the screams
The dead would be walking through their minds
They would never forgot those terrible times.

The blind the gassed the limbless and shot
Those men who they treated never forgot
With courage and skill the Roses gave all
The work it was hard it gave no rest at all.

Some Roses were lost to the enemy fire
Some went insane eyes filled with a fire
Some died of exhaustion and terrible strain
More came across on the narrow gauge train.

They called them the roses of no man's land
Those angels of mercy in that foreign land
Who died with the soldiers while holding their hands
In that terrible place where man slaughtered man.

It's Sunday, one of those days when all you want to do is nothing. *Fairport Convention* are playing on the CD player, the sun is shining. Gin and tonic rules. Listening to the music I am again taken back to the early seventies. Dress code would be flowing *Laura Ashley* dresses, and multi coloured waistcoats, hair was long, days were longer, the chat was always political, or who had recorded what and what was it like. I remember the times we used to have in the folk clubs and all the lazy days spent with those who only wanted to have the world at peace. Friends came to visit, they brought their twin girls, gin and tonic is the order, so we sat and listened to the twins chatting away in their own private language, marvelling at the understanding they had for each other, the day was at peace, pity the world was not.

I am not a great lover of babies. I would prefer to see children when they can hold a reasonable conversation and their own cup, about ten years old is ideal. When they are babies they demand so much attention and looking after. They cost a small fortune in prams, clothes, nappies and baby food, and when you have fed them they throw up all over you, ungrateful little sods. They attract all the relatives who swoon over them saying, 'doesn't it look like so and so, and it's got its mother's eyes, and father's nose.' What a load of tosh, babies look red and wrinkled and look like themselves. Then comes the pram pushing, what an experience that is, you spend most of the time stopping for nosy old bats to peer in the pram, breathing germs all over baby in order to make it ill and keep you awake even more than it usually does. Then there are the toys, teddy bears that give baby asthma, small toys it can shove up its nose, bigger toys it chucks at the television causing near heart attacks, and the constant sterilising and nappy washing. And the clothes, hundreds of baby clothes, it will be grown up before it can wear most of them. But for all that we wouldn't be without them. Or would we? No.

The saying goes, 'you can choose your friends, but you can't choose your family,' how true that saying is. I have one sister who runs a family of, it seems like, dozens each time I see her there seems to be another addition, either a cat, dog or child has joined the fold. Her main loves are her countless cats, they seem to be in every nook and cranny, then the dogs, they will either sit on you, lie on you or bite you. There are birds in cages and things that swim in tanks, staring out at you. Her home is like a zoo, everyone is welcome, animal or human, although it is sometimes difficult to distinguish between them, the house is never empty. Peter, her husband, has a full time job serving tea. Which he does with great panache and excellent timing between rolling cigarettes and shouting at the animals to get down or out. Life is full and hectic, you can be assured of a welcome and a seat providing the tortoise is not taking afternoon tea on the sofa. All the local gossip accompanies the tea between barks growls and meows.

If you have had a pet, you never seem to be without them, they leave hairs on everything, they constantly demand feeding, they have to be exercised, taken to the vet when ill, which costs a fortune, you clean their mess, you bath them and you break your heart when something happens to them, and all you get is constant affection from the first feed me call at 5am to lights out. From cats who are so aloof and seem not to need you, to the dog that is constantly at your side, we can't seem to get away from them. I have always had a dog, but when the last dog I had died, her name was Zoë, I couldn't put any of us through the pain we went through again. Zoë had been with us for fourteen years and it was a very sad day when she died. I think people who like cats are a bit special, their whole mood is quieter and more relaxed. If you are feeling stress, (that is the in word for wound up) try stroking a cat, it really does calm you down, providing the cat in question is not digging its claws into your leg or trying to savage your hand. Horses have a calming effect as well but you can't get one on your lap.

It's the 27th of September 2004. We have lost Mr Podge.

Mr Podge has been with us for sixteen years, he was a ginger tomcat who had such a personality. He never said much when he was with us, the occasional meow, or growl and hiss but for the greatest part of his life he was silent. The last few days of his life however, he did speak. I think he was telling us he was not well and that the inevitable was very close. He spent most of the few remaining days with us very close and if he could manage he would sleep under the bench beside the waterfall in the garden, we decided to place his ashes there, so he would be with us when we're there.

How strange, it's only a cat, but he was not a cat he was a friend a friend who was with us for sixteen years, the attachment was very strong.

MR. PODGE

I have a ginger tomcat
His name is Mr. Podge
My mum says he will burst one day
And leave a nasty splodge.
He gets up every morning
And stuffs himself with food
And then he wobbles back to bed
Making noises very rude.

GINGER TOM

For sixteen years, we had him that silly ginger tom
He never caused us trouble or strayed away from home
He was the boss in his small world and kept the dogs at bay
And laid out in the sunshine almost every day.

We have two other tomcats a Baggins and a Sprat
However, none can hold a candle to Podge the ginger cat
Fearless as a tiger with the cunning of a fox
He always slept upon the bed never in a box.

It's hard to say goodbye to him he was a part of us
He always sat beside you for a bit of fuss
He tried to trip you up as you passed him on the stair
And when we had our supper he sat upon his chair.

Tit bits we would feed him until he had his fill
Then he made his way outside and climbed his little hill
To settle underneath his bench and burp away his tea
And listen to the waterfall and have his evening sleep.

So goodbye Mr Podge you were the best of cats
So silly in a lot of ways but never nasty spats
You kept us all amused and followed us about
It going to be very hard now you are not around.

Chapter Ten

It had been seventeen years since I had heard from Vicky or Hugh. Any attempt at contact was rebuked until one day a letter arrived from Vicky asking if I was ever in Scotland could I call and see her. She gave her address in Glasgow, not my favourite town, however, I was lorry driving at that time and was frequently in Scotland, so off I set. And with an understanding boss managed to get a day in Glasgow to visit Vicky.

I found her after much searching through the great sprawl that is Glasgow, this town held only bad memories for me. In 1969 I was badly beaten up after stepping off a bus near Tobreck Street, I have never forgotten this incident. Vicky was living in a flat with her husband, Steven, a big gentle man and during the short time I spent with him I deduced him to be a good solid man who would look after his family. They were expecting their first baby, I was so shocked but at the same time so happy that I had found her. I expected to see a little girl not a fully-grown woman, the shock knocked me back somewhat. Where had my little girl gone? The smile was still there and the colouring but these now belonged to a young woman, not my Vicky, not the little girl I used to call Digel.

She cooked me ham and chips, a traditional meal for visitors in Scotland it's the solid old standby meal. We sat and talked firstly about her and her life that I had missed, we talked of her mother Anne, and how she was now coping with her problem, it then came out why she wanted to see me. I must admit feeling a bit disappointed that she had an ulterior motive for getting in touch, but her concerns were very real.

Hugh, who she protected as much as she could was giving her

cause for concern, he was living in a caravan with his girl friend. She was concerned that he was smoking marijuana, not a lot, but enough to make Vicky worried. She had seen her mother's addiction with alcohol take control of her life and she was worried that the same thing was happening to Hugh. She could not go to her mother with the problem and her only hope was that I could help, maybe making restitution for my past misgivings, that was providing Hugh would see me.

I, of course, agreed to try and help, bearing in mind these two young adults, although they will always be children to me, were total strangers and the thought of alienating them by interfering in their lives worried me. I had long awaited an opportunity to try and re-acquaint myself with them both and this was the best chance I was ever going to get. Thankfully I had a very understanding boss who arranged a load to Aberdeen and then on to Forres, way up north, to pick up a load and spend the weekend with Hugh. Steven's parents live in Forres, so Vicky and Steven were going to stay with them. We were all going to meet there. All went well, Wendy came up with me. Kirk stayed with Wendy's mum, his newfound grandma and made Welsh cakes and was spoiled rotten.

The weekend was a little strained as Hugh was not at ease with the situation and Vicky was not at ease with Wendy, but after a while they seemed to warm to us and I arranged that on my next trip to Scotland Hugh was going to meet me in Aberdeen and come to stay with us for a while.

The plan worked, Hugh came to stay and seemed settled, although after a week or so we did notice changes in him. He would go out each evening about nine, when he came back after about an hour he was different. He was a lot more talkative, it was not long before it became apparent he had found a dealer and was back on the dope. I must admit I hoped it was just a passing phase but I was so wrong.

Then it happened, Wendy found a letter written by Hugh to his stepfather, drugs were mentioned, she also found a substance, which turned out to be cannabis, so she hit the roof. Kirk was ten years old then. Wendy quite rightly did not want drugs in the house. I was in Scotland with my truck at the time this all happened. Wendy telephoned me to tell me what had taken place and I had to agree with her. Hugh walked out and unfortunately now wants nothing to do with us. I am so sad about this and have tried to talk to him but he is like me – stubborn. I do keep in touch with Vicky, not as much as I would wish, but she has a life of her own and if she ever needs me I will be here for her as I would for Hugh or Kirk. It's a pity we can't turn time around, just a bit. Kirk was very upset that Hugh had left, he had found a new brother and was very fond of him.

When Anne deposited Vicky and Hugh on us all those years ago it did not become apparent why, until I had a call from Vicky in 2003. She sent a message to say she wanted to see me, not in Scotland, but at my mother's home in Llandrindod Wells. Vicky's children were ten and eleven years old at this time. When I saw Vicky at mother's the hair on the back of my neck stood on end, she looked so much like her mother at first I thought it was her.

When the initial greetings were done we went for a walk, it was then she asked me if I had ever opened a box that had been locked for many years only to discover that the contents were so horrible that the reason for locking it suddenly became apparent? She told me the story of how she and Hugh had suffered abuse from the man Anne had married, Charles Smith, and since divorced. I was horrified, Vicky told me of the torment she and Hugh had gone through at the hands of this man, all I wanted to do was to kill him and had it not been for Wendy I would have and I freely admit this. I would have committed murder. I have never felt such hatred as I did for this creature. When I got back home that evening I talked to Wendy about what Vicky had told me, I was so upset and I do blame myself for the terror they must have gone through.

After a couple of days soul searching, still wanting to go to Scotland and kill this creature who had taken my children's innocence, I managed to write a letter to Vicky, which was one of the hardest things I've ever had to do. All I wanted to do was to hold her and Hugh and tell them how sorry I was for leaving them both to the torture they must have gone through, telling her to go to the police and report the abuse. With the help of a very understanding and loving husband, Steven, she did. I am so glad she has Steven, he so understands and he too wants this creature sorted out, but was wise enough not to get physically involved with him.

Just a codicil to end this story, the creature that pretended to be a father to my children, but gave them nothing but torment hung himself on October 24th 2003. A fitting end for a coward who was afraid to face the consequences of his action. Hugh has become somewhat of a recluse. He wants nothing to do with me, I can't say I blame him. It is a sad fact Vicky and Hugh will never be able to forgive me for abandoning them to the mercy of their abuser, I can't blame them, only myself.

LOST

I lost my kids some years ago
I wasn't there to see them grow
I thought about them every day
And how I used to watch them play.

The pain was bad the times were hard
My kids were in a far off land
Growing up without their dad
I bet they felt so lost and sad.

One girl, one boy a family
They really meant a lot to me
I wish that I could turn the tide
To keep them both I really tried.

But things do not work out that way
And so they went so far away
Out of reach and out of sight
To cry alone each long night.

I've found the one she is so fair
With two sons her life to share
I hope it works out fine for her
Her man will always care for her.

But with my son the tide will turn
And maybe he will want to learn
That all I have for him is love
I cannot give him more.

Life is sometimes hard, it deals out the cards and expects us to play them, no matter what, and success depends on the breaks, not those that sometimes fall into your lap, but the ones you make yourself. These are the most difficult, you strive to get things right then when things seem to be settled and everything is chugging along smoothly, someone, or thing, happens to throw a spanner in the works, what's the saying, 'life's a bitch and then you die.'

I can't stand cruelty to animals or children. I get very upset when I see anything that can't defend itself from being abused and I am of the belief, that anybody who gets pleasure from inflicting misery on any living thing is very badly deranged. We live in such a problematic society, and to some violence and abuse seem to be the normal way of things.

I find these people pathetic and sickening. I blame the media for a lot of the problems, when I was young if you saw a body on the television, due to war or violence, it would horrify you. Today you sit and eat you dinner while watching people being mown down in some war or other and not turn a hair, how low can we sink. I realise we have to be informed of such events but could there be more of a watershed for such matters, so as not to let youngsters see what the so called adults do to each other.

The same could be applied to video games for children and cartoons. Why is it they all have to kill, just about all the cartoons watched are about killing or destroying, it's time a censor who is worth their salt took a firm grip on this industry. Have you ever heard the phrase 'your dancing on a pin head' well it means that you are taking too many chances so I think I had better get back on to a lighter note before I fall off my pin head.

Wendy and I have taken to travelling, whenever we get a spare week, that is not very often as we both work, but sometimes a week will present itself and away we go. I must say I do love to travel I never thought I would but to see other countries is such an experience I would recommend it to every one. My family never travelled except to the shops, sad.

The world is big but it is getting smaller thanks to new technology and faster aircraft. I could never get my mother to travel abroad, she maintained if God had wanted her to fly she would have been born with wings and if he wanted her to cross the sea she would have been a fish what adventures she has missed.

STOP AT HOME

My mother never travelled, she was too scared you see
By air she would not venture, nor across the briny sea
I feel she missed out on so much, not travelling around
She should really fly away, but she won't get off the ground.

Travelling by motorcar, she has no fear at all
But try to get her on a boat, she won't have that at all
I can't swim is her excuse, and neither can I fly
Flying is for the birds, and my feet will stay dry.

I wish she would try flying, or sailing on the sea
But to get her on the go, is very hard you see
To venture on an aeroplane, and take a flight to Spain
I'm sure that she would like it and want to go again.

Jake was another acquaintance of mine, he was not what one could call dishonest but if an opportunity presented itself Jake would take advantage of it, he had served sometime in the army and had reached the dizzy heights of lance corporal and as such he had also landed himself a very cushy job in the officers' mess. But Jake looked this gift horse in the mouth once too often and landed himself into the shit up to his neck, he served some time in the army prison based in Colchester and when his time was up he was asked to leave the service of her majesty. So Jake started up in the junk business avoiding work as much as possible, I often said to him if he worked as hard at a job as he had avoiding one he would be a millionaire.

I don't think Jake was lazy but he had an aversion to work, he had got himself into the system where the social security was keeping him and his family. He would claim for anything they needed but he always maintained it was his right as he had served his time in the army and been kicked out over a slight misunderstanding, so he intended to carry on with his lifestyle and get as much out of the government as he could, he did make a good living.

JAKE

Jake was always nicking, it was his favourite game,
Football, rugby, cricket, were games that were too tame
To chance his arm against the law, was all that Jake did need
So when he stole a loaf of bread, some butter he did need.

He broke into the grocers, some butter for to nick
But as he passed the counter, his conscious gave a prick
He stopped himself and thought awhile about the deeds he'd done
But then he took the butter and started off to run.

As he ran a voice called out, "I know it's you young Jake
And if I ever catch you, I'll scalp you with a rake.'
And as young Jake was running, a thought to him occurred
I nicked the blooming butter, but forgot the lemon curd.

The next day came a knocking at young Jake's door
PC Plod was standing there, with the owner of the store
'That's him', the grocer cried, tugging at Jake's ear
PC Plod, the kindly soul said, what all is this here.

Jake was taken into court, to face the local beak
And told you are a naughty lad, your future looks quite bleak
Jake was thinking quick now on how best to make things right
He said it was not me my lord, I was playing on my bike.

At this outburst the beak did say, you're probably quite right
Because the bike you ride is blue you stole it from my wife
I think you are a good lad, that's strayed into bad ways
So I'll place you on probation, and hope you mend your ways.

So Jake was on probation and treatment was prescribed
A psychiatrist was advised for him, at this he nearly cried
So Jake went to the sessions, twice weekly, was the rule
Jake had got himself into this and he really felt a fool.

Jake went to see this doctor for a hundred weeks or more
And at the end of this time, they thought he had been cured
When Jake went to the final meet, they asked him please to wait
He thought about the good old days, and stole a paper weight.

Now Jake is very sorry, for all of his misdeeds
In fact he is quite reformed, and thinks of other's needs
He doesn't nick much any more, it isn't so much fun
When you're on a dessert island and you're the only one.

When we bought our new house it was nothing but a concrete slab, the walls were still in packs stacked up on the slab. It was our first brand new home, it seemed to take months to build and when it was completed we had to do what is called a snagging list, that is to list any faults for the contractors to put right, I must say the standard of work left a lot to be desired and as such it took a full two years to get the house somewhere near right.

RIP OFFS

The system is so old you see, I can't get all the parts
And all the pipes are rusted and the gutters are all blocked
That window frame is rotten and the down pipe has come loose
And to get a ladder round the back, we'll have to go over the roof.

The patio is a disaster and will have to be re-laid
The cost of bricks and mortar, you will be so amazed
The brickwork all needs pointing and that door's to be replaced
I don't know how you live here, this place is a disgrace.

Whatever were you thinking when you bought this shack
I'd find your estate agent and make him take it back
The wiring's shot, the plumbing's crap, the kitchen's a disgrace
I cannot understand you, buying such a place.

My answer to all his quips was fairly to the point
If tradesmen did an honest job and did not make mistakes
I wouldn't need your services, or your stories to be told
Because you see this fine old house, is only six months old.

We love our house and Wendy has taken control of the garden as well as the garage, which she uses as an office. I am left with my own little room where I keep my books and musical instruments, which are many, although I can't play any. I am a hoarder I can't help it I collect all sorts of things from badges to bugles, I am a magpie for shiny objects or even objects that don't shine.

STUFF

They say the things you gather, tell a tale of you
Everything from pictures that you never view
Books that gather dust and papers, old and torn
Clothes out of fashion and shoes rarely worn
We can't throw them out, or give them away
For they may come in handy on a rainy day.
Boxes full of ornaments, packed away so tight
Albums full of photos that never see the light
Records that are never played, from a time gone past
Everything from trumpets to a cobbler's last
Life would be so empty, if things we did not keep
So never, let the thought of it, disturb you in your sleep

The house looks out over Caerphilly, there are green fields to the rear and beautiful views. My room where I spend more time than I should, is comfortable and somewhere I can shut myself off from the world outside. It is a retreat, it is so important to have a retreat of some sort where you can recharge and relax, somewhere away from all decision making and kitchen duties, which I hate so much. In America it would be known as a den, but that sound so animalistic I much prefer my room, my space, my retreat, sanctuary.

MY ROOM

I have a little room
It's where I sit and write
No space to swing a cat
In fact it is quite tight.
A window to look out of
A telly for some noise
Watching through a window
At birds as they fly by.

I sometimes write a poem
Stories come sometimes
I'm glad I have my little room
It keeps me occupied.

Kitchen duties have always terrified me as I don't have the patience to wait for anything to be cooked. My ideal would be to order my food and be able to eat it when I want it, not having to make my mind up what I want to eat and then have to cook it. I think I am really designed for hotel living, I particularly hate barbecues, I can't see the point of lighting a fire and in all probability burning yourself as well as the food, then standing over intolerable heat waiting to get things the colour of soot, then to have to get out all sorts of additives in order to disguise the taste of something unrecognisable.

When you add the extras you realise you have just swallowed a ball of fire, then you realise you have overdone the Tabasco. You dive for the water and trip over the cat and crack your head on the barbecue spilling the fire all over yourself and find yourself in accident and emergency with third degree burns. Would it not be more civilised to live in a hotel.

TABASCO

A bottle so small it takes no space at all
It sits on the shelf taking care of itself
So still and obtuse it makes no excuse
For blowing your head through the wall.
The contents you see are like fire to free
And a spoonful you won't even take
If you should do this you will soon see
The bite is just like a snake
So better beware of Tabasco so red
It will warm you up just you see
Don't lose your head never drink it in bed
And remember don't put it in tea

It's no good for the hair and gives breath an air
Spilled on carpets it leaves big red spots
So drink if you dare you will be so despaired
Spilled on shoes they eventually rot.

I have written a few poems about daily occurrences but in order to understand these I have had to delve into areas I have been trying to avoid.

Writing this book has been sometimes very difficult, not for the story but having to stop myself being too critical of the world we live in and the problems we face in our daily lives. We tend to take things for granted, if it does not affect us we take little or no notice.

The beggar in the street, do we contribute to his tin he holds out expectantly or do we pass him by criticising the state he has sunk to.

BEGGAR

With staring eyes and cider breath
They ask for change to help their health
A cup of tea or a bag of chips
They look at you with trembling lips.

You know they'll spend it all on booze
Curl in doorways, have a snooze
Wake when drink has left them cold
So off again sad stories told.

What makes a person sink so low
Why has he got no home to go
Are we the ones to try him save
Or will we take him to his grave.

Take pity on this beggar then
Give some small token in his tin
Don't turn your back and walk away
It could be you one sad day.

Do we actively pursue our Members of Parliament to try and improve our lot or do we let them carry on in their own sweet way ignoring the masses as they seem to do.

POWER

The halls of power they call to them
Those who pretend to call you friend
The politicians who canvas votes
And hide beneath long black cloaks.

The smile they give you at the door
The foot that's jamming in the door
The promises they make to you
There better off flushed down the loo.

Sticky handshakes pleading eyes
Only serve to hide the lies
I will do this and I will do that
Oh what a charming little cat.

Remember now on polling day
The cross against the honest name
And I will do the best for you
I have a very clever crew.

But if you have any sense
Be like most sit on the fence
Someone someday will come along
And sing a very honest song.

And he will surely get your vote
And he won't wear a long black cloak
And his foot won't jam the door
But no one's perfect anymore.

When we drive in our cars and see flowers placed on the side of the road where someone has met their untimely end do we slow down or just shrug it off as just one of those things.

FLOWERS

Flowers on a grass verge,
A message washed in rain
Memories of a lost one,
A victim of our time,
A grass verge filled with pain.

Flowers on a pavement
We see them every day
Nothing left but sorrow
Time cannot repay
A pavement filled with pain.

Flowers on a lamppost
Tied so neat and tight
See the flowers shadow
In the dim sad light
A lamppost filled with pain.

Flowers on a coffin
In a big black car
Travelling to a graveyard
The last trip's not too far
A black car filled with pain.

Flowers on a grave
Feel the tragic loss
Soil sprinkled hands
A small wooden cross
A grave that's full of pain.

When thugs beat up and rob do we actively pursue them through the courts or just let them off with a slap on the wrist.

HOODIES

We see them each and every day
The hoodies that come out to play
To steal and rob and chase around
They are blight upon our towns.

They slink in shadows every night
They jump at us and give us fright
They run and snatch at ladies bags
And mug the old call them slags.

I hope one day the same they get
And hope the frights never forget
I wish them ill these hoodie sods
And hope there captured by the plod.

Do we take our litter home or discard it on the street making the excuse that it keeps people in work. Do we clean up after our dog has fouled the footpath or walk away mumbling to ourselves I hope I don't tread in that.

POO

Pile it here pile it there we have no room at all
Piled up high searching sky this poo is wall to wall
All our waste thrown out in haste scattered all around
Under the hedge in the field and buried in the ground.

What shall we do with all this poo give it to the sea
When all the oceans are full of poo no more ships to see
muddy sludge and stinking mud dead things all around
what a way to end it all on man's disgusting ground.

So make a start to clean this earth or no more it shall be
try to tidy up the ground and don't forget the sea
Every time you chuck poo out remember this small rhyme
killing all that's good and clean don't chuck it out next time.

We all criticise the royal family from time to time but would we be without Queen Betty, and her entourage.

QUEEN BETTY

Betty the Queen is quite often seen
at the races or on her estates
She waves very prim and motions to him
That's Philip who stands by and waits.

She rarely does smile but give her a while
And a smile will light up her face
The smile that she shows will turn up your toes
And give your old heart a wee race.

Along with bands at the cenotaph still
To pay tribute to those who have gone

Everyone still in November's cold chill
Queen Betty is there standing strong.

Each Christmas at three we all stop to see
Queen Betty as she speaks to the nation
She tells of a year that may bring a tear
Bur steadfast she stands by her station.

At dinners and balls with Philip so tall
And sometimes a son at her side
She talks to them all even the small
And has a few gins on the side.

The police force could do with a shake up especially when it comes to paperwork, why can't they be more like the TV Tec's a bit more ruthless and a free hand.

TECS

Sherlock Holmes is the best
Though Poriot is not bad
Miss Marples is cunning one
Colombo makes you mad.

Frost is always righteous
Bergerac so slow
Magrait always smoked a pipe
Shaft as black as coal.

Madigan was very hard
Rockford makes you swoon
Sam spade was the hissing one
Kojak was the loon.

Morse was always very flash
While Lewis always had the cash

Dick Tracy always got his man
Jeeves with Worcester was the man.

Sitting at a pavement bar one day with a few friends enjoying the afternoon sunshine, we watched a young lady come out of the bar in a bit of a rush. She had been having an argument with her friend and it was evident that the argument had reached an impasse.

The friend who remained unmoved on her barstool watched her friend depart and walk down the street very much the worst for wear brought on by too much time at the bar. As she stumbled out onto the street she was struggling to stand on very high heel shoes, she stopped for a moment to take her bearings, she was very attractive and was dressed in a mini skirt that barely covered her lower regions, this invited lots of comments from the assembled company and lots of leering eyes followed her as she set off down the road. As she started to walk away the sound of her shoes on the pavement reminded me of a horse clip clopping. She had left her friend still sitting in the bar, they had evidently disagreed about something, a lover maybe. Her friend had lit a cigarette and as the smoke swirled around her hair, the girl was making unsteady progress down the street pausing to take a rear glance to see if her friend was following and satisfying herself she was not, continued on her way. Her friend at the bar was probably thinking of the past few hours or the coming few hours she was oblivious to all around her and carried on with her drink and smoke. The girl who had been clip clopping rather unsteadily slipped and fell twisting her ankle as she went down. Several young men rushed to help, no doubt in a hands on attempt to help her up, seeing she was very shaken and in much pain, one of the rescuers took out his mobile phone and rang the ambulance service. I never realised how difficult it was to call an ambulance, when the ambulance number was connected there seemed to be rather a lot of questions to answer, much; 'hold the line please', and, 'is the patient breathing and conscious?' 'Is she bleeding, can she stand?'

Eventually the ambulance arrived, the paramedic who took

immediate charge and asked all those who were helping to give her some air, that he now had things under control. It suddenly struck me how we now rely so much on our mobile phones and we would be lost without them, it would be like leaving home without your comfort blanket, the mobile phone has become your best pal, your lifeline, your grip on reality.

HEELS

Clippity clop clippity clop
On her way to the shops
Sexy heels, legs so long
Tapping out her merry song.

Clippity clop clippity clop
Never stopping no time for talk
Got to get the daily bread
Lots of thoughts in her head.

Clippity clop clippity clop
Rushing forward never stops
Doesn't have the time of day
Planning how to get her way.

Clippity clop clippity clop
Off to the pub drop of pop
Going home slightly drunk
Fall and ends up in a lump.

Cloppity clip cloppity clip
What a silly little slip
Broken heel twisted foot
Rest up now shoes no good.

BAR FLY

Waiting for the lover that may never come
Thinking of the future, sitting in the sun
Cigarette smoke swirling, twirling high
And sweet red wine at your side.

Dreaming of what could have been
But this life has been so cruel
Knowing what you should have been
If you weren't such a fool.

Now you're sitting in a bar
Thinking of life's pain
Sipping at your sweet red wine
Which should be best champagne.

Wondering if you came back,
Would you walk this way again?
Would you try and change it all
Or would it be the same.

PAL

Life without my mobile phone would be very dull
Nobody to talk to, nothing to fill the lull
No dirty jokes on the text, no messages at all
Life would be so boring; you'd climb the bloody wall
So please don't take my mobile, it's really all I have
I do so need to have it close, it is my only pal.

PLEASE HOLD THE LINE

With all the best intentions you use the telephone
Checking on your bank account to save a trip to town
Or try to get the gas board that is a work of art
Electric and the water cause a flutter of the heart.

Try to ring the taxman such an illusive guy
Your call it is important, so please stay on line
And if you are successful, the message that is heard
Just listen to our music it helps to calm your nerves.

When after twenty minutes, the line it goes quite dead
So with a finger shaking, you have to dial again
The message still repeats and the process goes ahead
Please press one for so and so, so here you go again.

Then suddenly as if by magic, a human voice you hear
They listen to your problem and silence follows on
You're on the wrong extension, and everyone's gone home
But if you ring tomorrow I'll see what can be done.

Those faceless voices on the line, those you never see
Say the same things all the time, voices never change
You hang up all frustrated, shaking with such rage
Then next day you phone again, it starts off just the same.

All our lines are busy, you're in a waiting cue
Your head it starts spinning you're not sure what to do
Your patience is exhausted the tune gets up your nose
Whyever did you bother, goodness only knows.

On a visit to New York we were lucky enough to pay a visit to the famous *Cotton Club* in Harlem, this is a jazz club where all the greats either played or visited. It was very glitzy, not as big as I thought it would be but it was so welcoming, we had a soul food supper with several very large gin and tonics and were treated to a wonderful evening of music and dance, we even sang on stage, not too many Welsh people can boast that. During the evening I was transfixed by the saxophonist playing in the band, he seemed to play with no effort at all, so when the club was closing I went over to talk to him and say how much I enjoyed the evening, also telling him I had got a saxophone and was finding it very hard to blow, he told me to go to a music shop on 45th Street and ask the man for a rovner. I did not want to show my ignorance and thanked him for his advice. Next day I went to the music shop and asked for a rovner. I was handed a small box which contained a rubber ligature for attaching the reed to the mouthpiece, this has in fact made the blowing of my sax much easier. I was so relieved I had a dread I was going to be the butt for some sort of joke.

New York was a wonderful experience, we also visited a gospel meeting in Harlem, this was a real treat, the singing was excellent the people were so welcoming and friendly and it was a joy to be part of this church service, whether you believe or not it was memorable.

SAXOPHONE

I love to blow my saxophone
It makes me feel so good
Although it's made of brass
It's classified as wood.

The curves it has enthral me
Lithe and sexy in its feel
Some of them are made of brass
Some are made of steel.

The sound that comes so sweetly
From its bell shaped horn
Makes your hair begin to curl
And makes you feel forlorn

I love to blow my saxophone
And hear its notes so clear
If only I could play it right
Instead of just by ear.

One other very memorable happening in my life, apart from getting married and the birth of my children, was the time I saw Frank Sinatra, Sammy Davis Jnr and Liza Minelli at the Albert Hall in London. It was spectacular, the music and song came up to every expectation it was a fantastic night, one I will always remember, especially as Frank Sinatra actually waved and winked at me, well that's my story. I have always been an avid fan of Sinatra and that night there was only me in that hall listening to him sing. I was amazed to see so much booze there was on the stage and Sammy and Frank were never without a drink and cigarette all the time they were on stage, but this added to the atmosphere. I don't know what they were drinking but they seemed quite happy with whatever it was and consumed many glasses through the performance.

THE VOICE

The Albert Hall has emptied I'm sitting in my seat
Lights are dim and steady, one sound my tapping feet
The stage holds all its magic, orchestra ready to strike
The conductor flicks fantastic and music fills the night

Overture over on stage slowly not much haste
Stands alone, thoughts his own, a smile upon his face
Blue eyes flash in the spotlight shoes softly walk to the mike
He looked up at me sat in my seat and sang for me that night.

All three of those very famous performers have had periods in their lives when they thought they had been deserted by their fans, they got too big at one time or another and forgot they were mere mortals. Then came the realisation everyone reaches at some point in their lives everybody needs somebody, even if it's just to tell them they are getting too big for their boots, just a little jolt to get them back on terra firma, and sometimes this jolt becomes a big bump.

INDECISIVE

If you believe in heaven, you must believe in hell
Or you don't believe in anything that is very well
But if you don't believe, what else is there to do
Just go carefully though your life, I'm sure that it will

HAVE ONE ON ME

Some they like a brandy, others thrive on port
Some a pint of beer's best, others take a snort
I like gin and tonic, her majesty likes wine
My advise to all of you is have a drink sometimes.

Some they drink the Stella, that is very strong
Try a bloody Mary, that won't last that long
Pernod is a quick fix that will blow your mind
Sherry is a lady's drink, it treats you very kind.

Cider makes you merry except the Scrumpy jack
Take a pint or two of this and you'll be on your back
Rum well that's a sailor's drink, a mainbrace for to splice
But when it comes to Christmas try mead it's full of spice.

Amaretto's very nice, also Cointreau orange full
Tequila sunrise oh so good best when it is cool
Vodka drives you crazy when it's taken neat
Martini is a nice drink always very sweet.

Never drink the water unless it's bottled stuff
The trouble with the water it always tastes of fluff
Whisky with the water the flavour you will lose
Whisky with the water is for the weak kneed fools.

The thing that makes performers great is the way they treat the audience, some have a knack of getting to the heart of an audience others have no idea at all. They believe if they sing loud enough and dress outrageously enough they will make it in the music industry, thank goodness they do not. So just a little advice for those who think they are the greatest, look how the old timers did it and try to emulate them just a little.

SOFT LANDING

To try and make it in this world
And get your name in lights
You have to do some silly thing
Such as acting and the like
And if you make it very big
And reach those dizzy heights
Be careful how you handle it
The ropes are very tight
If the rope should break on you
Make sure your landings soft
Because at the bottom
It's along way from the top

It's time to finish my little book at least for the time being, I have tried to tell the story as truthfully as I can. I feel that we live in a fast changing world that is full of people, good and bad, to the bad ones I hope they see the error of their ways to the good try to help the bad ones. Don't ignore the poor and forgive those who have dumped on you it may be time for the revolution, I firmly believe there will be one.

SING

A little thought for people, who think that they can sing.
And guitarists who play all the tunes, and never pluck a string
Try to learn the words and you won't have to mime
Then maybe music radio, will play you from time to time.

Try to find a mirror, before you start your act
And don't hide your features under a silly hat
Always please your audience, treat them with respect
Or invites from the telly, I doubt you'll ever get.

Wendy and I will have been married for thirty years on the 18th of December 2006 God willing and a fair breeze. It has not all been easy we have had hard times we have had good times. I have regrets, I have done things I am not proud of, I would be a liar not to admit this, so to all those I hurt I am sorry, but life does not always take its planned route and deviations sometime have to be taken, no matter how risky, some get hurt along the way that is life, we have to get on with it.

It may be time for the revolution I firmly believe that there will be one, I hope it will be a small one but effective.

POWER TO THE PEOPLE

It may be the time to turn the tide,
And get out of this plight,
To vote out all the wastes of time
And start to put thing right,

It's time to take it in our hands
And try to fight the fight,
Whitehall is the powerhouse
But it's very rarely right.
So let's put on the marching boots
And trundle down that road,

And relieve all those pretenders
Of their very heavy load,
I know it sound like treason
But this is not the case,
If they can't listen to reason
Then they're just a waste of space,
Try a coalition it couldn't really hurt
Then cut down all their wages,
I'm sure that this would hurt
Chuck out all the wasters,
Make them sweep the roads
Try to live on our pay,
It's a very lonely road
So listen all you rulers,
Try to get things right
Or you may find yourself
Sleeping rough tonight

CURTAINS

Keep all your curtains tightly closed
To keep you safe and warm
Watch out for the gaps and chinks
Those robbers are abroad

They look into to your privacy
And spy into your life
They peep at you each morning
But mostly through the night
They spy at all your goodies
They plan to steal away
And flog them at the boot sale
They never work for pay

Draw your curtains every night
They'll keep the robbers away
For they will steal all your goods
Instead of earning pay

FIRST KISS

The planning and the heartache and shaking of the hands
When it comes to the crunch you forget what you have planned
How should you approach it you would welcome any tips
A kiss as sweet as best red wine that lingers on your lips.

You miss her lips the first time and feel a little shamed
You've lost that wondrous moment so you try again
The pursing of the lips goes wrong you dive in like a twit
The shaking hands and nerves all gone, after oh! that bliss

WRITER'S BLOCK

The whiteness of the paper
No lines of ink appear
No mark upon the foolscap
No fingers on the keys

The block has come to haunt you
Staring blank and stark
Try to sleep to get inspired
And all you get is dark

You toss and turn to try and think
Anything to flow the ink
You wake up in an empty mind
To write those words you cannot find.

You may just write a masterpiece
Or just some silly rhyme
Getting those first few words
They always tear your mind

So if you want to be a writer
And pound those keys all day
Don't give up on your day job
You'll have to earn some pay

BYE, BYE

Now I think it's time to go
So I will wish you cheerio
I hope your life will be fulfilled
And of good stuff you get your fill
So if you're ever down my way
Any month or any day
Please call in don't be chronic
Call in and have a gin and tonic.

I hope whoever reads this will read the rhymes and poems in context as they tell their own story.